麦格希 中英双语阅读文库

难忘的旅程

【美】富尔顿 (Fulton, L.) ●主编

匡颖　刘慧●译

麦格希中英双语阅读文库编委会●编

全国百佳图书出版单位
吉林出版集团股份有限公司

图书在版编目（CIP）数据

难忘的旅程 / (美) 富尔顿 (Fulton,L.) 主编；麦格希中英双语阅读文库编委会编；匡颖, 刘慧译. -- 2版. -- 长春：吉林出版集团股份有限公司, 2018.3
（2022.1重印）
（麦格希中英双语阅读文库）
ISBN 978-7-5581-4785-2

Ⅰ. ①难… Ⅱ. ①富… ②麦… ③匡… ④刘… Ⅲ. ①英语—汉语—对照读物②世界史—文化史—青少年读物 Ⅳ. ①H319.4：K

中国版本图书馆CIP数据核字(2018)第046412号

难忘的旅程

编：麦格希中英双语阅读文库编委会
插　　画：齐　航　李延霞
责任编辑：孙琳琳
封面设计：冯冯翼
开　　本：660mm×960mm　1/16
字　　数：167千字
印　　张：9.75
版　　次：2018年3月第2版
印　　次：2022年1月第2次印刷

出　　版：吉林出版集团股份有限公司
发　　行：吉林出版集团外语教育有限公司
地　　址：长春市福祉大路5788号龙腾国际大厦B座7层
　　　　　邮编：130011
电　　话：总编办：0431-81629929
　　　　　发行部：0431-81629927　0431-81629921(Fax)
印　　刷：北京一鑫印务有限责任公司

ISBN 978-7-5581-4785-2　　　定价：35.00元

前 言 *PREFACE*

英国思想家培根说过：阅读使人深刻。阅读的真正目的是获取信息，开拓视野和陶冶情操。从语言学习的角度来说，学习语言若没有大量阅读就如隔靴搔痒，因为阅读中的语言是最丰富、最灵活、最具表现力、最符合生活情景的，同时读物中的情节、故事引人入胜，进而能充分调动读者的阅读兴趣，培养读者的文学修养，至此，语言的学习水到渠成。

"麦格希中英双语阅读文库"在世界范围内选材，涉及科普、社会文化、文学名著、传奇故事、成长励志等多个系列，充分满足英语学习者课外阅读之所需，在阅读中学习英语、提高能力。

◎难度适中

本套图书充分照顾读者的英语学习阶段和水平，从读者的阅读兴趣出发，以难易适中的英语语言为立足点，选材精心、编排合理。

◎精品荟萃

本套图书注重经典阅读与实用阅读并举。既包含国内外脍炙人口、耳熟能详的美文，又包含科普、人文、故事、励志类等多学科的精彩文章。

◎功能实用

本套图书充分体现了双语阅读的功能和优势，充分考虑到读者课外阅读的方便，超出核心词表的词汇均出现在使其意义明显的语境之中，并标注释义。

鉴于编者水平有限，凡不周之处，谬误之处，皆欢迎批评教正。

我们真心地希望本套图书承载的文化知识和英语阅读的策略对提高读者的英语著作欣赏水平和英语运用能力有所裨益。

丛书编委会

Contents

1

Seven Wonders of the Modern World

Picking Wonders

Long ago, scholars selected the seven greatest works built by human beings—the Seven Wonders of the *Ancient* World. These wonders honored the courage and power to do things people thought couldn't be done. The Great Pyramid of Egypt is the only Ancient Wonder still standing.

Hundreds of years later, a group of engineers asked experts around the world to select seven new wonders. Their list of Modern

---

现代文明七大奇迹

奇迹的评选

在很久以前，学者们选出了人类建筑史上的七项最伟大工程——称为"古代文明七大奇迹"。这些奇迹体现出古代人民挑战不可想象之事的勇气与力量。在"古代文明七大奇迹"中，只有埃及大金字塔完整保存至今。

数百年后，全球众多专家应一组工程师之邀，评选出新的七大奇迹。

---

ancient *adj.* 古代的；远古的

Wonders honored the same ideas as the Ancient Wonders.

- Channel *Tunnel* (England/France)

- Netherlands North Sea Protection Works (Netherlands)

- Canadian National Tower (Toronto, Canada)

- Empire State Building (New York City, United States)

- Golden Gate Bridge (San Francisco, United States)

- Panama Canal (Panama)

- Itaipú Dam (Brazil/Paraguay)

Channel Tunnel

Let's start in England and France. Imagine traveling 31 miles

---

他们所选出的"现代奇迹"与"古代奇迹"体现出相同的代表意义。

英法海底隧道(英国/法国)

荷兰北海保护工程(荷兰)

加拿大国家电视塔(加拿大多伦多)

帝国大厦(美国纽约)

金门大桥(美国旧金山)

巴拿马运河(巴拿马)

伊泰普大坝(巴西/巴拉圭)

英法海底隧道

此次旅行让我们从英法启程。设想要以每小时100英里的速度穿过一

---

tunnel *n.* 地下通道；隧道；地道

through an underwater tunnel at *close to* 100 miles per hour. The Channel Tunnel, or Chunnel, provides speedy travel between England and France. The trip takes about 20 minutes.

People had dreamed of this tunnel for years. The work was hard and risky. It took about 13,000 people from 1987 to 1994 to build three tunnels a total of 95 miles long. First, workers dug huge *chunks* of chalk and clay from the bottom of the English Channel. Then they built the tunnels under the water!

Passengers can now ride through the Chunnel in buses and cars that are loaded onto the widest trains ever built. One tunnel allows train travel from England to France while a second allows travel in

---

条水下通道，行走31英里。英法海底隧道就在英、法两国之间提供了一条这样的快速通道。全程需要约20分钟。

多年来，人们一直梦想有这样一条隧道。隧道建造工程艰险重重。从1987年到1994年，大约13 000名工人的辛苦努力打造出总长为95英里的三条隧道。起初，工人们在英吉利海峡底部挖掘大量的泥灰质白垩岩。然后他们就在水下建造出了隧道！

乘客们现在可以乘汽车或轿车通过隧道，这些车辆装载于海底隧道列车之内，这些列车也是世界上最宽的列车。三条隧道中的一条从英国开往

---

close to　（在空间或时间上）接近　　　　　　　　　　chunk　n.　大量

the *opposite* direction. The third tunnel is a service tunnel used for repairs and *emergencies*.

A couple of years after the Chunnel opened, a fire started in one of the tunnels. A fire could have killed many, but the Channel Tunnel had plans for emergencies.

People were taken off the train and led to the tunnel used for repairs and emergencies. Some people became sick from the smoke and were taken to the hospital. However, no one died or was seriously hurt. The safety plans saved the day.

Netherlands North Sea Protection Works

Now let's travel north from France to the Netherlands, where

法国；另一条从法国开往英国；第三条是服务隧道，用于修缮或应对紧急情况。

在海底隧道开通几年之后，其中一条隧道起火。火灾本来会使许多人丧生，但海底隧道对此情况早有应对策略。

当时车上的乘客被转移出列车，改乘用于修缮和应急的那条隧道。有部分乘客因为浓烟而感觉不适被送往医院。但没有人丧生或受重伤。正是这些应急方案发挥了作用。

荷兰北海保护工程

现在我们从法国向北进发到达荷兰。荷兰的大部分土地都在海平面以

opposite *adj.* 相反的　　　　　　emergency *n.* 紧急事件；紧急情况

much of the land is below sea level. During storms, floods destroyed homes and farmland. In the early 1900s, the Dutch suffered the effects of war and terrible storms. Food shortages were a problem. They decided to find new ways to protect the land and people from the sea.

In 1927, the people started to build the North Sea Protection Works. They *dammed* areas along the coast to create lakes and farmland.

Floodwalls keep surges of water during storms from flooding the land.

But other areas couldn't be dammed. More dams would hurt the country's shipping industry and wildlife *habitats*. So they built a

---

下。在风暴来袭时，洪水毁坏了家园和农田。在20世纪早期，荷兰人饱受战争之苦，风暴袭击也令他们苦不堪言。食物匮乏也是一大问题。于是荷兰人决定寻找新的方法保护家园，保护人们免受海洋的侵袭。

1927年，人们开始建造"北海保护工程"。他们围绕海岸筑起大坝，开发出湖泊和农田。

防洪墙在风暴来袭时可以挡住洪水，保护土地。

但是有些地区无法筑坝。如果筑坝过多，将会对荷兰的航运业，野生动植物的生存环境造成不利的影响。所以，人们建造出一条不同于以往

---

dam *v.* 建水坝于 　　　　　　　　　habitat *n.* 自然环境；栖息地

floodwall unlike any other. The wall was built with *giant* gates that stay open when the sea is calm. This allows ships to come and go and keeps the wildlife safe. During storms, the gates can be closed to prevent flooding.

The North Sea Protection Works gave the Dutch over one-half million *acres* of land for farming, livestock, and homes. The people also gained protection from floods.

Canadian National Tower

Next we cross the Atlantic Ocean from the Netherlands to Toronto, Canada, where visitors can stand on an observation deck of the Canadian National, or CN, Tower and see Niagara Falls, about 85 miles away. Over 1,800 feet high, the tower is the tallest *freestanding* structure in the world.

的防洪墙。这道护墙带有巨大的闸门，如果海面平静，闸门就处于开放状态。这样船只来去自由，也保护了野生动植物。如果风暴来袭，闸门即可关闭，预防洪灾。

"北海保护工程"使荷兰人拥有了超过50万亩的土地，用于耕种、畜牧，建造家园。即使洪水来袭，人们也可以得到保护。

加拿大国家电视塔

接下来，我们从荷兰穿过大西洋来到加拿大的多伦多。在这里，游客们可以站在加拿大国家电视塔（又称CN塔）的瞭望台上看到85英里以外的尼亚加拉大瀑布。加拿大国家电视塔高达1 800英尺，是世界上最高的独立式建筑。

---

giant *adj.* 巨大的　　　　　　　　　　　　　acre *n.* 英亩
freestanding *adj.* 无支撑物的；不固于某物上的

In the 1960s, Toronto had built many tall buildings. Many were so tall they blocked radio and television signals. The city needed a tower tall enough so that no building could block signals coming from it. Plans were drawn up for the CN Tower.

Building something so tall was not easy. Workers used *instruments* on planes flown over the CN Tower to make sure it was straight. Builders used a helicopter to place the *antenna* at the tower's top. Around the tower's base, they constructed a four-level observation deck that was lifted into place high above the ground when it was finished. The top level, Skypod, is the highest public observation deck in the world.

20世纪60年代，许多高大的建筑在多伦多拔地而起。其中许多因为过高而挡住了电台和电视台的信号。多伦多需要一座高塔，其高度要超过其他建筑，这样信号传播就不会再受阻。于是，人们开始构想加拿大国家电视塔。

要建造这么高的塔绝非易事。工人们需要在飞机上，在飞过CN塔时使用仪器确保塔的垂直度。建造者利用直升机在塔顶放置天线。在塔基周围，他们盖起了四层的瞭望台，在塔竣工之时他们将瞭望台脱离地面建到高处。最顶层的瞭望台叫作"天空之盖"，是全世界最高的公共瞭望台。

instrument *n.* 器具；仪器   antenna *n.* 天线

The Tower is a popular tourist attraction. On the bottom observation level, The Glass Floor, visitors walk on a see-through surface and look down at the city below.

Empire State Building

We move southeast of the CN Tower to the Empire State Building in the United States. Started in 1930, it was the tallest building of its time and rose in the New York City skyline in one year and 45 days.

Construction began during the Great Depression. Many people were looking for jobs, so they didn't mind the danger and hard work of building it so quickly. They built four and one-half floors a week, and put together the 58,000-ton *frame* in less than a month.

这座塔现在已经成为广受欢迎的旅游景点。在**瞭**望台底层是玻璃地板，游客们可以透过透明的地板俯瞰城市景色。

帝国大厦

我们从CN塔向东南方向行进，就到达了美国的帝国大厦。帝国大厦始建于1930年，是同时代最高的建筑，整个工期仅用时1年零45天便在纽约空中拔地而起。

大厦的建筑开始于美国的经济大萧条时期。许多人没有工作，所以他们不怕危险，不计辛苦，只想快速完工。他们一周就可以盖完四层半楼，用了不到一个月就完成了重达58 000吨的大厦框架的架构。

---

construction *n.* 施工；建设

frame *n.* 框架

The 1,250-foot tall, 102-story building became a New York City *landmark*. It has 73 elevators, 1,860 steps, and 6,500 windows. People come from around the world to see the city from the observation deck.

Golden Gate Bridge

Traveling to the west coast of the United States, we find the Golden Gate Bridge in San Francisco. Local residents wanted a bridge across the narrow waterway between San Francisco Bay and the Pacific Ocean. After 65 years of planning, construction started in 1933, providing jobs during the Great Depression.

Men worked on towers 746 feet above the water. That's a little

---

这幢高达1 250英尺的102层高楼成了纽约的地标式建筑。大厦内有73架电梯，和6 500扇窗户，底层至顶层共有1 860级台阶。人们从世界各地赶来，只为了从大厦的瞭望台上一览纽约风貌。

金门大桥

沿美国的西海岸游览，就会看到旧金山的金门大桥。当年，当地居民想要一座桥，穿过旧金山与太平洋之间的狭窄水道。在65年的计划之后，大桥于1933年动工，当时适逢美国经济大萧条，这一工程为不少美国人提供了工作岗位。

工人们在水面以上746英尺的塔上劳动。这一高度甚至已经超出了帝

---

landmark *n.* 陆标；地标

more than half the height of the Empire State Building. The men worked with thick *cables* in *bundles* a yard wide. They worked in the cold, fog, and wind, and with the constant danger of falling. In fact, 11 men fell to their deaths while working on the bridge.

To build this type of bridge, workers first had to construct tall towers. Then they strung really strong and thick cables between the towers. The floor, or deck, of the bridge was hung from the cables. The cables were *secured*, or held in place, at each end of the bridge.

You can see the thousands of wires inside the cable being walked on (top) in the *cross-section* above.

国大厦的一半高。工人们要带着宽达一码的成捆缆绳在上面工作。工作环境冰冷、多雾、强风，而且随时有坠落的危险。而事实上，在大桥建造期间，有11名工人跌落身亡。

要建造这种吊桥，工人们首先要建造高塔。然后他们在高塔间挂起非常结实粗壮的缆绳，桥面要从这些缆绳上吊下去。在桥的每一端，这些缆绳都要确保其安全性，并固定好位置。

在大桥上方，可以看到成千上万根细钢索连接着大桥，供人们和车辆在桥面行走。

---

cable *n.* 缆绳；绳索
secure *v.* 保护；（使）获得

bundle *n.* 束、捆、扎或包在一起的东西
cross-section *n.* 横断面

On the day the Golden Gate Bridge opened in 1937, people walked its 4,200-foot length—that's almost a mile. The first cars traveled across the next day. Since then, over a billion and a half vehicles have used the bridge. Once the longest and tallest suspension bridge in the world, it is still one of the biggest and most *spectacular*. It has even survived a major earthquake.

Panama Canal

Our next stop is south of the United States in the country of Panama, where a lake almost connects the Atlantic and Pacific

---

1937年金门大桥开放的这一天，人们走过了全桥4 200英尺（接近一英里）的距离。首批过桥的汽车是在第二天通过大桥的。至今，已经有超过15亿的车辆通过大桥。金门大桥一度是世界上最长、最高的吊桥，现在它仍然是世界上最大、最壮观的桥梁之一。甚至在经历过一次严重的地震之后，大桥仍安然无恙。

巴拿马运河

我们的下一站是位于美国以南在巴拿马境内的一条河流，此河几乎

---

spectacular *adj.* 场面富丽的；壮观的

Oceans. As early as 1534, people talked about digging through the land to extend the lake to the oceans. Work started on the Panama Canal in 1904 and took 10 years to finish. Before the canal, people had to *sail* around South America to get from one ocean to the other.

During digging, disease, landslides, and *mudslides* caused problems. After they finished digging, they built a system of *chambers* to raise and lower ships from the oceans to the lake. Ships enter chambers on one side of the canal that take them to the lake. The ships make their way across the lake to chambers that will take them down to the ocean on the other side.

连接了大西洋与太平洋。早在1534年，人们就开始设想挖掘土地使这条河流延伸至海洋。巴拿马运河的建筑工作始于1904年，整个工程历时10年。在巴拿马运河竣工之前，人们需要绕道南美洲航行才能往返于太平洋与大西洋之间。

在挖掘期间，遭遇了许多难题，包括疾病、土地滑坡、泥石流等等。挖掘完成后，人们建造了若干个船闸来控制往来于海湖之间的船只的高低水位变化。船只进入运河一侧的船闸，从而进入湖泊。通过湖泊，这些船只就可以进入另一侧的船闸，然后进入海洋。

---

sail *v.* 航行；起航

chamber *n.* 室；内庭

mudslide *n.* 泥流；泥石流

Today, the canal can *handle* about 50 ships a day — it averages about 14,000 ships a year.

How the Panama Canal Works

1 A ship enters the canal chamber, where it will be raised from sea level to lake level.

2 Water flows into the chamber from the lake to make sure the water is the same height on both sides of the gate.

3 The gate opens and the ship moves into the lake.

There are three chambers on each side of the lake. This means that water flows from one chamber to the next three times to raise and lower the ships on each side.

目前，每天大约有50艘船通过运河，平均每年通过运河的船只大约有14 000只。

巴拿马运河是如何运作的

1 一艘船进入运河船闸，在这里船的水位由海平面高度上升至湖面高度。

2 水从湖里流进船闸，以确保在闸门两侧水位同高。

3 闸门打开，船向前移动进入湖中。

在湖的两侧各有三个船闸，这意味着船在每一侧上升和下移过程中，要经历三次水位高度的变化。

---

handle *v.* 应付；处理

Itaipu Dam

Now we head south from Panama to the countries of Brazil and Paraguay. In 1975, the two countries *teamed up* to build a *hydroelectric* plant to produce more electricity for their people. They would build it on the Paraná River, on the border between the two countries, because a hydroelectric plant needs water and a dam to create electricity.

Builders overcame big challenges. They changed the *course* of the Paraná, the seventh largest river in the world. They dug up and removed more than 50 million tons of dirt and rocks. They used enough *concrete* to build a city for four million people and enough iron and steel to build 380 Eiffel Towers.

伊泰普大坝

从巴拿马运河向南，便到达了巴西和巴拉圭。1975年，这两个国家合力建造了一座水电站生产更多电力供人民使用。这座水电站坐落在两国交界的巴拉那河上，因为水电站需要水和大坝共同发电。

面对世界上第七大河——巴拉那河，建造者们克服了巨大挑战。他们改变了巴拉那河的河道，挖掘并移走了超过5 000万吨的灰土和岩石。建造水电站所使用的混凝土足够建造一座有400万人的城市，所使用的钢铁足够建造380座埃菲尔铁塔。

team up 与……组队；协作　　　　　　hydroelectric *adj.* 水力发电的
course *n.* 航向；航线；路线　　　　　concrete *n.* 混凝土

The result was a series of dams as well as a power plant one-half mile long. The power plant has broken records for the amount of power it produces. It now supplies most of the power for Paraguay and about a quarter of the power for Brazil.

How Does a Hydroelectric Plant Work?

The Itaipú Dam is a giant wall with gates that hold back water from the Paraná River. When the gates of the dam are opened water goes through a pipe to a *turbine*. The turbine has blades—like a fan, only much larger. The water makes the blades turn. The blades cause powerful *magnets* in the *generator* (something like a motor) to turn. When the magnets pass *copper* coils inside the generator,

---

最终，建成了一系列的大坝和长达半英里的水电站。这座水电站打破其发电总量的记录，现在负责巴拉圭国的大部分电量供应及巴西国内1/4的电量供应。

水力发电站是怎样工作的？

伊泰普大坝坝墙矗立，装配闸门，拦腰截断巴拉那河。当闸门开启，水流经过管道进入水轮机。水轮机带有叶片，状如风扇，但比风扇要大上许多倍。水流冲击带动叶片旋转。叶片带动发电机（如同引擎一样的东西）内的巨大磁铁开始旋转。这些磁铁旋转着通过发电机内的铜线圈，电

---

turbine *n.* 涡轮机
generator *n.* 发电机

magnet *n.* 磁体；磁石
copper *adj.* 铜制的

electrons get moved around. Electrons are tiny bits of energy. These electrons are turned into electricity.

Conclusion

Someday, new lists of wonders will be made. Works greater than these are already being built. However, these Seven Wonders of the Modern World are proof of the power and courage of human beings in the 1900s.

子开始移动。电子是小粒的能源。这些电子的移动最终产生电能。

小结

总有一天，人们会评选出新的世界奇迹。比目前这些奇迹更伟大的工程已经在建造之中。然而，"现代文明七大奇迹"则是20世纪以来人类力量与勇气的证明。

---

electron *n.* 电子

2

China

If you were to travel west to the edge of the Pacific Ocean, you'd come to Asia. Asia is the largest continent on the planet with more land and people than anywhere else in the world. Asia is also home to one of the biggest, most *diverse* countries in the world—China.

中国

如果你要到太平洋的西侧去旅行，你就会来到亚洲。亚洲是这个星球上最大的大陆，土地最大，人口最多。亚洲还有世界上最大、最为多元化的国家之———中国。

---

diverse *adj.* 形形色色的；各式各样的

China has an *incredible* mix of people, *landscapes*, and wildlife. It is the third largest country in the world (only Russia and Canada are bigger). And it has the largest population in the world. In fact, one out of every five people in the world lives in China— that's more than 1.3 billion people!

> **Do You Know?**
>
> China has more than 1,500 rivers—including some of the biggest rivers in the world. The longest river in China is the Yangtze (yank-SEE), which is the third longest river in the world. (Only the Amazon River in South America and the Nile River in Africa are longer!)

China is also a country alive with art, music, dance, food, and

---

中国的人口、地貌和野生生物非常复杂。中国是世界第三大国家（只次于俄罗斯和加拿大）。它是世界上人口最多的国家，实际上世界上5个人之中，就有一个人住在中国——超过13亿！

> **你知道吗?**
>
> 中国有1 500多支河流，其中一些是世界上最大的河流，中国的最长河流是长江，这是世界上第三长的河。（只次于南美的亚马孙河和非洲的尼罗河！）

中国的绘画、音乐、舞蹈、食物和庆典都充满活力，以丰富的文化圣

---

incredible *adj.* 不可思议的　　　　　　landscape *n.*　（陆上）风景；自然景色

celebrations. And it's known for amazing cultural sites—from temples and palaces to *statues*, canals, and the longest hand-built wall in the world.

The Chinese also have a long, rich history of learning and inventing. They were the first people to make and use paper, ink, writing, silk cloth, printing, kites, *porcelain*, gunpowder, the *compass*, and much more.

The Great Wall of China

More than 2,000 years ago, the first emperor of China, Qin Shi Huangdi, started building the Great Wall. It was designed to keep *hostile* tribes from invading China. The Great Wall, which was mostly built by slaves, is the longest wall in the world. It's also the largest

---

地而闻名——有庙宇、宫殿，还有雕像、运河和世界上最长的、人工修建的墙。

中国人的学识与发明有着悠久丰富的历史，他们最先制作和使用纸张、墨水、书法、丝绸、印刷、风筝、瓷器、火药、指南针等许许多多。

中国的长城

2 000多年前，中国的第一个皇帝，秦始皇，开始建造长城，防范敌对的部落入侵中国。长城大都是由奴隶来建造的，现在是世界上最长的墙，也是人工建造的最大的建筑物。全长6 437公里（4 000英里），长城

---

statue *n.* 雕像；雕塑
compass *n.* 指南针；罗盘

porcelain *n.* 瓷
hostile *adj.* 敌对的；敌人的

structure ever built by hand. It is more than 6,437 kilometers (4,000 miles) long. It was built wide enough so as many as 10 soldiers could march side by side when they patrolled the countryside. It's so big, it can be seen from a space *shuttle orbiting* Earth! Although parts of the Great Wall are crumbling, you can still see many of the more than 20,000 watch towers that served as look-out points thousands of years ago. The Great Wall crosses northern China between the east coast and north-central China.

Wild China

One thing that makes China special is that it has many different kinds of natural places. There are rugged mountain peaks, rocky deserts, tropical forests, and *lush* valleys.

的宽度很大，可容下10个士兵在乡间巡逻时并肩行走。长城非常宏伟，可以从绕地球飞行的航天飞机中看到。尽管长城的某些部分正在倒塌，你还可以见到20 000多个遗留了几千年的瞭望塔，这是几千年前用来放哨的地点。长城横穿中国北部地区，介于东海岸和华北中部之间。

野生的中国

一件让中国很特别的东西是它有很多不同的天然的地方，有崎岖的山峰，遍布岩石的沙漠，热带雨林和繁茂的峡谷。

---

structure *n.* 建筑物
orbit *v.* 环绕轨道运行

shuttle *n.* 飞机
lush *adj.* 繁密的

And because China is such a big country with so many different habitats, it has many different kinds of living things. There are giant pandas in the bamboo forests of central China. There are tigers and monkeys in the tropical forests in the south. And there are all kinds of animals and plants that live in and near China's many rivers and streams— including the giant *salamander*.

Giant Panda

The Chinese people are so proud of the giant panda that these animals have become a symbol of their country. Giant pandas live in the *steep* bamboo forests of China, feeding almost nonstop on these tall, quickgrowing grasses.

Many pandas will spend more than 16 hours a day eating

因为中国国土辽阔，有很多不同的栖息地，所以也有很多不同的生物，在华中的竹林里有大熊猫，在南部的雨林中有老虎和猴子。中国许多河流里和河流附近生活着各种各样的动物和植物——包括巨螈。

大熊猫

中国人对大熊猫非常自豪，它已经成为这个国家的象征。大熊猫生活在中国陡峭的竹林中，几乎一刻不停地吃着这种长得很高、很快的植物。

许多熊猫每天要吃至少16个小时的竹子，每年吃10 000磅。

---

salamander *n.* 蝾螈　　　　　　　　　　　　steep *adj.* 陡峭的

bamboo, or about 10,000 pounds in a year.

Scientists attempt to breed pandas in *captivity* to preserve the species.

Unfortunately, China's population has grown so quickly that many plants and animals are losing their habitats. For example, scientists say there are fewer than 1,000 pandas left in the wild. The bamboo forests where pandas live are being cut down for farming and houses.

Chinese Characters

In addition to many natural treasures, China has a rich culture filled with special celebrations, art, music, dance, sports, and food. If you visit China, one of the first artistic things you might notice is

---

科学家试图在人工饲养条件下繁殖熊猫，以保护该物种。

非常遗憾，中国人口增长得很快，很多动植物已经失去了栖息地。例如科学家们说，野生状态下的熊猫不足1 000只，它们生活的竹林也被砍倒，用于耕地和建房。

中国的汉字

除了很多的自然宝藏外，中国还有丰富的文化，包括特别的庆祝活动、美术、音乐、舞蹈、体育和食品。如果你到访中国，你可能注意到的

---

captivity *n.* 圈养；关押

the writing. The official language of China is *Mandarin*, which uses more than 6,000 characters instead of the 26-letter *alphabet* used in the English language. Each character stands for a word or a part of a word.

Here are the Mandarin characters for:

Fire mountain forest woman

Lunar Calendar

Year of the...

RAT OX TIGER RABBIT DRAGON SNAKE HORSE SHEEP MONKEY ROOSTER DOG *BOAR*

Each Chinese year is named after one of 12 animals. It repeats every 12 years. Look at the calendar to find the animal name for the year you were born.

第一件艺术品就是书法。中国的官方语言是普通话，共有6 000多个汉字，而不是英语中使用的26个字母，每个汉字表示一个词，或一个词的一部分。

下面是汉语的几个汉字

火、山、森林、女人

农历

鼠年、牛年、虎年、兔年、龙年、蛇年、马年、羊年、猴年、鸡年、狗年、猪年。

中国年的每一个年都用12个动物中的一个命名，12年一个轮回，看看这个日历，查出你出生时的动物年。

Mandarin *n.* 普通话

lunar *adj.* 阴历的

alphabet *n.* 字母表；全部字母

boar *n.* 公猪；野猪

Celebrating China: From Dragons to Food

If you visit in late January or early February, you might be lucky enough to take part in the celebration of the New Year. This is one of China's most important festivals and is celebrated throughout the country.

To celebrate the New Year, people take part in colorful parades, wearing bright *costumes* and often dressing up as dragons. The dragon is a sign of good luck in China. Fireworks are also a big part of the festivities.

Many people ride bikes to get around China's *congested* cities.

Sports are also important to the Chinese. You'll probably see a lot of people playing table tennis (Ping-Pong™). The Chinese are some of the best table tennis players in the world! You'll also see a lot of bike riders, since most people get around by bike.

庆典中的中国：从龙到食物

如果你在一月下旬或二月上旬访问中国，你可能会有幸参加新年庆祝活动，这是中国最为重要的节日，举国上下同庆。

为了庆祝新年，人们会参加五彩缤纷的游行，穿上色彩鲜艳的服装，经常会打扮成龙的样子。龙在中国是一个吉祥的象征。烟花也是庆祝活动的重要部分。

在中国拥挤的城市中，很多人骑自行车出行。

体育对中国人来说也很重要，你可能会看到很多人打乒乓球 ，中国人里面拥有一批世界上最优秀的乒乓球选手，你还会看到很多骑自行车的

---

costume *n.* 戏服；表演服   congest *v.* 充满；拥挤

Food and Chinese culture go hand in hand. If you've eaten in a Chinese restaurant, then you know that there are many flavors and spices that make Chinese food special. Different regions of China are known for different kinds of food. For example, food from southwestern China is very spicy and often uses chili pepper oil. You might also notice that the Chinese only use two *utensils*: chopsticks and a soup spoon.

The Chinese eat a lot of rice. Rice is grown in flooded fields called paddies. In many parts of China, rice is served with all meals and is an important part of the Chinese diet. You'll also see people eating noodles, soups, fish, soybeans, and other foods.

人，因为中国人大多数骑自行车出行。

食物与中国文化密不可分。如果你在中国餐馆中吃过饭，你就会知道中国饭菜之所以特殊是因为它有很多的风味和很多的调料。中国不同的地区以不同的食物而闻名，例如，中国的西南部地区食物以辣为主，经常使用辣椒油。你可能也注意到中国人只使用两种餐具，筷子和汤勺。

中国吃大米吃得多一些，水稻种在灌有水的田地里，叫作水田。在中国很多的地方，每餐都有米饭，它是中国人一种非常重要的食物，你也能看到人们食用面条、汤、鱼、大豆和其他食品。

---

utensil *n.* 器具；用具

> ## Do You Know?
>
> The Chinese eat three times more fish than Americans. In fact, the average person in China eats more than 20 kilograms (45 lbs) of seafood each year.

China has a long and rich history, which has helped shape the country today. Most historians think the country was settled more than 5,500 years ago—making China one of the earliest civilizations in the world that is still *thriving* today.

The capital of China is Beijing (BAY-jing). It is a city of almost 14 million people. Beijing is the center of government. It is also known for its many tourist sites, like Tiananmen Square, also named the

---

> ### 你知道吗?
>
> 中国人吃鱼的数量比美国人多三倍, 事实上, 中国人每年人均食用海产品为20公斤 (45磅)。

中国有着悠久和丰富的历史, 对今天的中国有很大的影响。大多数的历史学家认为, 这个国家在5 500年前就已经安定下来, 成为世界上最早的人类文明, 今天仍很繁荣。

中国的首都是北京, 这里有1 400万人口, 北京是政权的中心。北京以旅游地众多而闻名, 例如天安门广场, 也叫天安门, 这个大广场位于城

---

thriving *adj.* 兴旺的; 旺盛的; 繁荣的

Gate of Heavenly Peace—a large square in the city's center that is used for special events.

China also has many other thriving cities. Shanghai (shang-HI) is the largest city in China and one of the biggest ports in the world. And Hong Kong, in the southern part of China, is a major business center known for its many shops and markets.

Even though many of China's more than 100 million people live in cities, most people still live in rural towns and villages. Many of them are farmers to herd sheep and goats in the grasslands.

Land of the Silk Moth

Most of the world's silk is produced in China. Silk comes from the *caterpillar* of a silk moth—the only *domesticated* insect in the world.

市的中心，用于一些特别的活动。

中国还有很多其他充满活动的城市。上海是中国最大的城市，也是世界上最大港口之一，香港位于中国的南部，是一个主要的商业中心，以众多的商店和市场而闻名。

尽管中国有一亿人口生活在城市，更多的人口仍生活在农村乡镇或村庄中，他们的许多人是在草地上放牧绵羊或山羊的农民。

丝绸之乡

世界上的丝绸大部分产于中国，丝绸来自蚕蛾的幼虫，是世界上唯一

---

caterpillar *n.* 毛虫　　　　　　　domesticated *adj.* （指动物）被驯养了的

The caterpillar *spins* a silken cocoon, and people harvest the silk threads from the cocoon. The Chinese discovered silk about 2640 B.C., and kept it a secret for almost 3,000 years.

Today, China has the second largest economy in the world. It is a leader in making and selling many products to other countries— from toys to televisions and *textiles*, such as silk. It also has a huge tourist industry and was picked to host the 2008 Olympics in Beijing.

But China faces big challenges. Recent reforms by the Communist government mean more private businesses will grow. The move away from a system where everyone works for the government means China has many *unemployed* workers. The "opening up" of the economy is expected to be better in the long term, but this kind of change does not come easily.

家庭养殖的昆虫。幼虫吐丝织出蚕茧，人们从蚕茧上收获蚕丝。中国人在公元前2640年发明了丝绸，这个秘密保持了近3 000年。

今天的中国是世界第二大经济体，它是产品制造与出口他国的领军者——从玩具到电视，以及诸如丝绸的纺织品等等。它还有庞大的旅游业，并被选为举办2008北京奥运会主办国。

但是中国也面临着很大的挑战，最近由共产党政府发起的改革，意味着中国私有企业将要增长，这是摆脱人人为政府工作的体制，也就是意味着很多人的失业，这种开放的经济，从长远看会有更好的效果，但这种变化并非唾手可得。

---

spin *v.* 吐（丝）；作（茧）   textile *n.* 纺织品；织物；纺织业
unemployed *adj.* 被解雇的；失业的

As China's population grows, people will need more water, energy, food, and other *resources*. The country faces the challenge of providing enough jobs and resources for its population while still protecting the environment and people's rights.

随着中国人口的增长，人们需要更多的水、能源、食物和其他的资源。国家面临着为这些人口提供充足就业和资源的挑战，还要保护环境和人民的权益。

resource *n.* 资源

Ancient Egypt

Introduction

Hundreds of years ago, a group of people lived in the African country of Egypt. They lived on the banks of the Nile River. They were farmers and hunters. They used the river for boat travel. They were *ruled* by a king called a pharaoh.

古 埃 及

引言

几百年前，有一群人住在埃及这个非洲国家，他们住在尼罗河的两岸，以种田和打猎为生。他们利用河流乘船出行，他们受国王即法老的统治。

---

rule *v.* 统治；规定

Beliefs

The ancient Egyptians believed that after someone died, he or she went to live in another world. They believed that a person's next life would be like their present life. They thought the dead person would need the same *tools* and objects in their next life. So people were buried with many of the things that they owned.

Ancient Egyptians believed in a sun god. They believed that the king was *related to* this god. When the king died,he was given a very *fancy* burial. Many riches were buried with him. Queens were also given fancy burials.

信仰

古埃及人认为，人死了以后会到另一个世界生活，他们认为人的来生与今生很相似，来生中会使用相同的工具和物品，所以人在死后埋葬时同时也会埋下他原来拥有的东西。

古埃及人信太阳神，他们认为国王与神是有关系的。国王死了以后，会有一个非常豪华的葬礼。很多财宝会与他一起下葬，王后也会有豪华的葬礼。

tool *n.* 器具；工具　　　　related to 同……有关系
fancy *adj.* 奇特的；昂贵的

After a king died, his body was preserved so that it would not *rot*. People believed that this would keep his *spirit* alive. The preserved body was called a mummy.

Pyramids

The king was buried inside a huge stone structure called a pyramid. The pyramid was shaped to look like the sun's rays shining on Earth. People believed that the king would go to heaven on the rays of the sun.

Pyramids took many years to build. When a king was still alive, people began building his pyramid. The stones used to make the pyramid were huge. It took hard work to get the stones out of the

---

国王死后，他的尸体会被保存起来，让他不会腐烂。人们认为这样做他的灵魂还会活着，保存好的尸体被叫作"木乃伊"。

金字塔

国王被葬在一个叫作金字塔的巨大石建筑物里面，金字塔的形状很像太阳照射地球的光线。人们认为国王借着太阳光线会升入天堂。

金字塔需要很多年才能建起来。国王在世的时候，人们就开始为他建立金字塔。用来建金字塔的石头很大，把它们从地面弄到高处是很不容易

---

rot *v.* （使）腐烂；变质　　　　　　　　　spirit *n.* 精神；心灵

ground. It took where the pyramid would be built. Some stones were moved on boats. Other stones were moved over land using big *sleds*.

Inside the pyramid was a tomb. This was a special room where the king's body was placed. Many objects were put in the tomb. There were statues, paintings, and many gold things.

Many hidden tunnels and rooms were built inside a pyramid. They were built to *trick* anyone who tried to *steal* things from the tomb. Giant stones were put in front of the doorway of the real tomb. They were used to keep out thieves. Still, almost every king's tomb has been *robbed* over the years. But the pyramids still stand.

The Great Pyramid at Giza is a famous pyramid. It was built for King Khufu. It has more than 2 million blocks of stone. Other

---

的。把石头运到建立金字塔的地方更加不容易，有的石头是用船来运送，有的则是用大的雪橇在陆地上运送的。

金字塔的里面是墓穴，这是一个专用于放置国王尸体的地方。墓穴内还有很多其他东西，有雕像、画作和很多金器。

金字塔里面建有很多的暗道和房间，目的是混淆来偷东西盗墓者的判断。在通往真正墓穴的门前放置有巨大的石头，用来阻拦盗墓者。但是几乎所有的国王的墓穴都被盗过，只有金字塔还矗立着。

吉萨的大金字塔是最有名的，是为胡夫王修建的，共用了超过200万块石头。周围的金字塔是为国王的亲戚们修的，一个被称作斯芬克司的雕

---

sled *n.* 雪橇
steal *v.* 偷；窃取

trick *v.* 欺骗
rob *v.* 抢夺；抢劫

pyramids near it were built for the king's relatives. A statue called the Sphinx *guards* all of the pyramids. The Sphinx has the face of a king and the body of a lion.

Conclusion

Studying the ancient Egyptians teaches us a lot about life long ago. We can learn about the tools these people used and clothes they wore. We can learn about the food they ate and the gods they *worshipped*. By studying ancient Egyptians, we know that they had a great culture.

像，守卫着这些金字塔。斯芬克司拥有国王的脸孔和狮子的身体。

结语

通过研究古埃及人我们可以了解到很早以前人们的生活：我们能够了解到这些人用过的工具，穿过的衣服；我们还知道了他们吃的食物；他们信仰的神。通过研究古埃及人，我们知道他们拥有过很伟大灿烂的文化。

---

guard *v.* 守卫；守护

worship *v.* 崇拜；崇敬

Castles

What Is a Castle?

During the Middle Ages, many great castles were built across Europe. The castles were made to protect people from their enemies. They had thick, tall walls and watchtowers where guards stood watch over the castle.

The people who lived in the castles were the *nobility*, or *nobles*.

城 堡

什么是城堡？

在中世纪，欧洲大陆上建起了很多著名的城堡。城堡是建来保护人们免受敌人的攻击的。城堡有着又高又厚的城墙和瞭望塔，哨望守卫在塔上看守整个城堡。

住在城堡里的人都是名人，或者贵族。但城堡内不只是住着他们，服侍和保护他们的人也住在里面。贵族们不只是住在城堡里，除了城堡他们

---

nobility *n.* 贵族（阶层）　　　　　　　　　　　　noble *n.* 尊贵的人

However, they were not the only people living in the castles. The people who served and protected the nobility also lived within the castle walls. The nobles not only owned and lived in the castle, they also owned much of the land *stretching* beyond the castle. They were *loyal to* the king. Their loyalty helped the king control even more land.

Living outside the castle was another class of people called commoners. They were the *craftsmen* and farmers who lived in small towns and villages and on farms not far from the castle. The commoners were loyal to the nobles. They paid taxes, which allowed the nobles to live *privileged* lives.

The First Castle

The first type of castle was called a mott and bailey. The mott

还拥有城堡外大片的土地，他们忠诚于国王，他们的忠诚有利于国王控制更多的土地。

住在城堡以外的人是另一个阶层的人，叫作平民，他们是手工艺者或农民，住在小镇子里、村庄里或者城堡附近的农场里。平民效忠于贵族，他们交税赋，贵族靠税赋过着享有特权的生活。

第一个城堡

第一种城堡叫作莫特和贝利城堡。莫特是一个很高的土堆，上面建有

stretch *v.* 延伸；绵延

craftsman *n.* 工匠；手工人

loyal to 忠诚于；忠于

privileged *adj.* 享有特权的；特许的

was a high mound of dirt with a wooden tower built upon it. A wooden fence, called a palisade, was built out from the mott. The palisade formed a wall surrounding the bailey, or the *yard* that held the *kitchen*, hall, stables, and other buildings belonging to the noble.

Later, castles had stone motts or towers. Many of these castles also featured moats. Moats were ditches, often filled with water, that surrounded the castle. As time passed, castles were built with bigger towers and walls. They became larger, with more rooms and passages. They came to look more and more like the large castles we see today.

一个木制的塔。一种木制的篱笆叫作栅栏，被沿着土堆建起。栅栏在堡场外，或者院子的周围形成一道墙，院子里有厨房、大厅、马厩和其他的建筑，所有这些都是属于那些贵族的。

后来城堡有了石头的莫特和塔，很多这样的城堡还有护城河，护城河就是绕城的沟渠，里面装满了水。随着时间的推移，城堡开始建起更大的塔和城墙。城堡本身也更大，里面有更多的房间和通道。越来越像我们今天看到的城堡的样子。

yard *n.* 院子

kitchen *n.* 厨房

Outside the Castle

Newly built castles were painted with a mixture of *lime* and water. This mixture gave the castle walls a fresh, clean coat of white. For this reason, the mixture was called whitewash.

Every castle's design was different. Still, they had many of the same features. Most had towers or turrets, and many castles had an inner and an outer wall. Many also had a very strong building in the center of the castle. This building was called a keep.

Many castles were built in places that made them easier to defend. Many were built in the middle of lakes or on *jagged* hilltops and cliffs. This made it hard for attackers to reach the castle.

城堡的外面

新建的城堡上面被涂上石灰和水的混合物。这层混合物会让城堡有一个清新、整洁的白色的外表。也就是这个原因，这种混合物被叫作粉刷。

每个城堡的设计都是不同的，但还有很多的共同特点。大多数都有瞭望塔或塔楼，很多的城堡都有内墙和外墙，中心都建有很坚固的建筑，这个建筑叫作主楼。

很多城堡都建在易于防守的位置，很多建在湖的中央或犬牙交错的山顶或悬崖上。这让攻击者很难接近城堡。

lime *n.* 石灰

jagged *adj.* 锐利的；有缺口的

The walls were often more than 3 meters (10 ft.) thick. The walls were topped with *crenelations*, or notches, that gave them a sawtooth look. This design protected archers from enemy arrows. It also made it more difficult to climb over the walls. The *primary* entrance was through the main gate. But often there were smaller gates around the castle's walls. These smaller gates were used for extra traffic or for deliveries to the kitchens.

Castles had many windows to let light in. This meant that fewer candles and torches would be needed to light the rooms and halls. Windows near the ground were *extremely* narrow so that attackers could not climb through them. Since windows high above the ground

---

城墙一般有3米（10英尺）厚，墙的上面是雉堞，或叫作凹口，所以看上去有一种锯齿的感觉，这样的设计可以保护弓箭手躲开敌人射出的箭。同样也给爬上城墙增加了难度。主要的入城通道是正门，但是城墙还会有小一些的门，这些小门被用于额外的交通或给厨房送货。

城堡有很多的窗户，用于采光，这样在房间或大厅里面就可以减少蜡烛和火把的用量。接近地面的窗户是非常窄小的，这样可以防止攻击者进到室内。因为离地面高一些的窗户不容易上来，所以窗户会大一些。大

---

crenelation *n.* 开垛口
extremely *adv.* 非常；极其

primary *adj.* 首要的；主要的

were difficult to reach, they could be bigger. Most of these larger windows had *shutters* to keep out bad weather and often had bars to keep invaders out.

The roofs and floors were made of hard wood. Many castles had cellars that were used to store food and wine. After the Middle Ages, *dungeons* were built in castle cellars. These dungeons were used to house prisoners.

Inside the Castle

Castles weren't just designed to be defended. They were also designed to make life comfortable for the nobles. One of the most important places in a castle was the Great Hall. It was where meals, *entertainment*, and *feasts* were held. It was also where everyone

---

多数的大窗户都有百叶窗，以应对坏天气，而且上面都有防止闯入者的栏杆。

房顶和地面都是用硬木做成的。很多城堡都有地窖，用来储存食物和酒。中世纪以后，在城堡地窖里还建了地牢，这些地牢用来关押犯人。

城堡内部

设计城堡不只是为了抵御攻击，还要为了让贵族们在里面生活的舒适。城堡里最为重要的一个地方就是大厅，它是进餐、娱乐和举行宴会的地方，也是大家聚在一起聊天或开会的地方。

---

shutter *n.* 百叶窗

entertainment *n.* 娱乐节目；娱乐活动

dungeon *n.* 地牢；土牢（城堡中的）

feast *n.* 宴会；筵席；盛宴

gathered to talk or hold meetings.

The kitchens were separated from the Great Hall by long passageways. Some kitchens were outside in another building to *avoid* the risk of the castles' wooden roofs catching fire. This meant that food for *medieval* feasts would arrive at the tables cold or wet with rain!

A castle had enough rooms to house the noble and his extended family. Visitors probably slept on straw mattresses in the Great Hall after the tables had been cleared away. Most castles had *spiral* staircases. They wound upward in a *clockwise* direction. They were built this way to slow down invaders by making it difficult to fight in the stairwells.

厨房与大厅是分开的，靠一个长长的走廊连接起来。有的厨房甚至是建在其他建筑里面，以消除城堡木制房顶起火的危险，这就意味着中世纪的宴会中，菜肴被端上桌子时可能已经凉了或者被雨水淋湿了。

城堡内的房间很多，足以容纳下贵族和他的家眷。外来的客人非常有可能在大厅的餐桌收拾利索后睡在这里的草垫子上。大多数的城堡都建有螺旋梯，上楼的方向是按照顺时针方向。这样的设计有利于防范入侵者，因为在楼梯中打斗是很困难的。

---

avoid *v.* 避开；避免
spiral *adj.* 螺旋状的

medieval *adj.* 中世纪的
clockwise *adj.* 顺时针的

Built for Defense

One of the most important things to consider in castle design was defense. A castle usually had two surrounding walls. The inner wall was taller than the outer one. Archers standing on the inner wall could fire their arrows over the defenders on the shorter wall. It also made it easier for those on the taller wall to defend against attackers who had reached the lower outer wall.

The two sets of gates on these walls often opened at opposite ends of the castle. This forced *invaders* to circle around the inside of the outer wall to find the other gate. While looking for the second gate, invaders could be hit by the castle guards' arrows.

Between the castle walls were the outer and inner wards. The

为防御而建

设计城堡中考虑的最重要因素是防守，城堡周围通常有两层城墙，内墙比外墙高，站在内墙的弓箭手可以越过矮一些的外墙上的守卫射箭。并且，如果入侵者到达了外墙，较高内墙上的人也很容易进行防守。

内外墙间的大门设在相对的方向，所以入侵者必须在内外墙间绕到对侧才能找到另一道城门。入侵者在找到第二道大门的途中，既有可能被城堡守卫的箭击中。

城堡的内外墙上有内外房。外房有店铺和房子，内房存有食物和武

---

invader *n.* 侵略者；侵入者

outer ward was filled with shops and houses. The inner ward was where the food and weapons were stored, the knights stayed, and water wells were dug.

In the center of the castle was a separate building called the keep. It was here that the nobility lived. It was the safest part of the castle and the hardest to enter. It was designed so that if the rest of the castle were *captured*, the nobles could still be defended.

During the Middle Ages, life *revolved around* the church. People believed that God gave the kings and nobles the power to rule. The church had at least as much power as the king. It represented the *authority* that gave the king his right to rule.

器，武士们也待在这里，这里还挖有水井。

在城堡的中央，有一个独立的建筑，叫作主楼。贵族住在这里，这是城堡里最安全的地方，也是最不容易进入的地方。它的设计是为了在城堡的其他部分被攻下时，贵族仍可以得到保护。

在中世纪，人们的生活主要是围绕着教堂的。人们认为上帝给了国王和贵族统治的权力。教堂的权力至少与国王是一样大的，它代表着给予国王统治权的权力。

capture *v.* 夺取；占领
authority *n.* 权威；权力

revolve around 围绕；以……为中心

The king and church had great power. They ruled everyone in the kingdom. Under the king and queen were several other classes of people. The highest class was the nobles. They paid the king a tax for the *privilege* to control land in his kingdom. The knights also ranked high in the kingdom. Below the knights were the *merchants* and artisans. And below them were the more common people such as *blacksmiths* and shoemakers. All of these people paid taxes to the nobles. They were allowed to hold land.

The lowest class was the peasants. They had to remain on the land where they were born. Peasants did not own land. These farmers had to give much of what they produced to the king and the

国王和教堂都有巨大的权力，他们统治着整个王国中的每一个人。在国王和王后的下面还有其他几个阶层的人。阶层最高的是贵族，他们向国王纳税，以取得管理、支配王国中土地的权力。武士在王国中也有比较高的地位，在武士的下面是商人和手工艺人，然后是平民，例如铁匠和鞋匠等，所有这些人都向贵族纳税，贵族允许他们掌管田地。

最下层的人是农民，他们必须待在他们出生的土地上。农民不能有自己的土地，他们必须把大部分收成交给国王和地主。

privilege *n.* 特权；权益
blacksmith *n.* 铁匠

merchant *n.* 商人

landowner.

Castles and War

Castles were the *targets* of many longrunning wars. Sometimes, walls were built around *entire* towns. The peasants would defend this town wall for as long as they could. If the town wall were overrun, then knights would defend the outer wall of the castle. If that fell, then the inner wall was defended. And lastly, the center building, or keep, that housed the nobles was defended.

Defending the castle was not easy. Enemies used many weapons to try to take over a castle. They used large battering rams to *hammer away at* the castle's walls and gates. They used weapons called

城堡和战争

城堡是很多长期战争的攻击目标。有时会在整个城镇的周围建起城墙，农民尽最大可能保护城墙。如果城墙被突破，武士们会保护城堡的外墙，如果城堡外墙也被攻破，内墙还有守卫。最后，中心建筑或主楼的守卫会继续保护住在里面的贵族。

守卫城堡不是一件容易的事情。敌人会使用很多的武器尽力攻占城堡，他们用大的攻城槌不断撞击城墙和大门，他们用一种叫弹射器的武器

target *n.* 对象；目标　　　　　　　　entire *adj.* 整个的；全部的
hammer away at 不断地做

catapults to *hurl* rocks, debris, and even dead animals or people over the walls. Giant slingshot-like weapons called trebuchets were also used to hurl objects over the walls. And to *discourage* the castle defenders from rushing out of the castle to attack them, the attackers used giant crossbows mounted on carts.

Many methods were used to keep attackers from entering a castle. Holes were cut into the floors of *arches* above the castle entrance. Defenders poured burning sand or tar on anyone trying to batter down the gates. Newer castles replaced arrow slits with keyhole-shaped windows where cannons could be placed.

Defenders use a catapult to repel an army that is using a siege tower. *Meanwhile*, soldiers tunnel underneath the moat and break into the castle.

拖着岩石、瓦砾，甚至是死的动物或人用力投掷进城里。有一种巨大的像弹弓一样的武器，叫作投石机，也被用来把物体投掷到城中。为了阻止城内防守者冲出城堡发起攻击，攻城者还会把巨大的弩装在车上面。

人们采用很多的方法防止攻城者进城。在城入口上方拱门的下面挖出洞，防守者把灼热的砂子或焦油从洞里倒在撞击城门的那些人身上。新建的城堡还把射箭孔换成了钥匙孔形的窗户，这样可以在那里架起大炮。

守城者用弹射器驱赶使用攻城塔攻城的军队。与此同时，攻城的士兵则在护城河下面打洞并进入城堡。

---

hurl *v.* 丢下；用力投掷
arch *n.* 弓形；拱门

discourage *v.* 阻碍；劝阻
meanwhile *adv.* 同时；期间

Moats made castles harder to attack.

The moat, often filled with water, surrounded the castle. It was difficult to tunnel under a moat, and attackers could not *wade* across the deep water. There is a *myth* that crocodiles were placed in the moats. Some moats did have eels and other kinds of fish in them for food, but there were no crocodiles.

Enemies also dug under castle walls to make them *collapse*. Sometimes they moved large wooden towers against a wall. They then used the towers to climb onto and over the walls. Attackers were known to use *portable* bridges, or barges, to cross the moat and attack a castle. But often it was not possible to break into a well-built and well-defended castle. So the attackers would simply wait

护城河的应用使攻城变得更加不易了。

护城河内通常是有水的，围绕在城堡的周围。在护城河的下面打开通道是非常不容易的，而且入侵者也不可能蹚水渡过深的地方。有一个神话说，人们在护城河里放了鳄鱼，有的护城河内确实养有鳗鱼还有一些其他鱼类用作食用，但并没有鳄鱼。

敌人也会用在城墙下面挖掘的方法来使城墙倒塌，有时还会搬来大的木塔靠在墙上，利用这种塔爬上或爬过城墙。现已经知道，攻城者采用轻便易携桥或驳船穿过护城河来攻打城堡。通常不太可能攻克建筑良好、防

wade *v.* 蹚；走过　　　　　　myth *n.* 神话
collapse *v.* 倒塌；塌下　　　　portable *adj.* 轻便的；便于携带的

for the castle's residents to *run out of* food or water.

Around the 1600s, castles became less and less popular. They were no longer easy to defend because of the use of heavy cannons in warfare. The nobles also wanted more comfortable and open places to live. Still, many castles stand today as a *reminder* of an age gone by.

守好的城堡，所以攻城者只是等着城内居住的人断粮或断水。

　　17世纪后，城堡越来越不受欢迎了，城堡的防守不再那么容易了，因为战争中使用了大炮等重型的武器。贵族们也想到一个更舒服、更开阔的地方居住。但今天还有很多的城堡矗立着，让人们忆起那已经远去的时代。

---

run out of 用光；用尽　　　　　　　　reminder n. 令人回忆起……的东西

5

C Is for Canada

Subject: *Greetings* from Canada

Hey Stephanie,

I t was so exciting to get your email yesterday! I've been *looking forward to* having a pen pal for some time now. I'm so glad your teacher in Omaha (that's in Nebraska, right?) contacted mine here in Vancouver (that's in British Columbia). Do you know

C代表加拿大

主题：来自加拿大的问候

亲爱的斯蒂芬妮：

昨天收到了你的邮件，真是太开心了。一直以来，我都期望能结交一位笔友。很高兴，虽然你的老师在奥马哈（属于内布拉斯加州，对吧？），她还是联系上了远在温哥华（属于大不列颠哥伦比亚省）的我的老师。你知道这是哪里吗？

---

greeting *n.* 问候；招呼；敬意   look forward to 期望；盼望

where that is?

British Columbia is one of the 10 provinces in Canada (there are three *territories*, too). We don't have states like the United States.

Anyway, in your last email, you said that you are doing a report on Canada. Is this the kind of information that you're looking for? If not, could you be more *specific*? I hope I can help.

Your Canadian pen pal,
Jacqueline

Subject: My questions

Hi Jacqueline,

Good to hear from you. Here, let me list some of the topics that my teacher wants *covered* in the report so that you have a better idea

---

大不列颠哥伦比亚省是加拿大（共有三个区）的10个省之一。我们不像美国以州为单位划分。

你来信提到你正在做一份关于加拿大的报告。以上信息是你所需要的吗？如果不是，能否把你的需要说得详细些？我希望能帮上忙。

来自加拿大的笔友
杰奎琳

主题：我的问题

杰奎琳：

你好！很高兴收到你的信。现在，我就列出一些老师希望我报告中涉及的话题，以便你更清楚地知道我需要哪些信息：人物、经济、政府、历

---

territory *n.* 属地；地区　　　　　specific *adj.* 详细的；特种的；特定的
cover *v.* 涉及；包括

of what information I am looking for: people, *economics*, government, history, culture, religion, and *physical* geography. Hope that's not too much.

So, what's your family like? My dad sells animal feed and my mom is a waitress at the truck stop outside of town. Do you have any brothers or sisters? I don't.

Thanks so much for doing this, and I can't wait to tell you about Omaha and the United States for your report next month.

Your friend,

Stephanie

Subject: My family

Hey Stephanie,

史、文化、宗教和自然地理。希望没有给你带去太多的麻烦。

对了，你的家庭是什么情况？我的爸爸做动物饲料生意，妈妈在城外的载货汽车停车场做服务员。你有兄弟姐妹吗？我是家里唯一的孩子。

再次感谢你为我做的一起，我也迫不及待地要向你介绍美国和奥哈马，希望能对你下个月的报告有所帮助。

你的朋友
斯蒂芬妮

主题：我的家庭
斯蒂芬妮：

---

economics *n.* 经济；经济体制   physical *adj.* 自然（界）的

Wow, that is a lot of information to cover! How about this: I'll start by talking about my family (that will at least cover your "people" *section*) and then maybe that will help answer some of the other sections. Okay?

My dad is a fisherman in English Bay. He leaves before I wake up for school because he says he has to get to the Bay before the fish wake up! Vancouver has the largest port in North America, as far as *exports* go. It also rarely *freezes*, so my dad works year-round.

Fish are a major resource here. My dad says Canada exports about 80 percent of its fish. Other resources are iron ore, nickel, zinc, copper, gold, silver, coal, and oil. I found that information online at Statistics Canada (you may want to check it out).

你好！哇，你要了解的内容还真是不少呀！那么，先从介绍我的家庭（这至少涉及你报告中"人物"部分的内容）开始吧，怎么样？而且，这也可能对回答其他部分的问题有所帮助。

我的父亲是格兰湾的渔民。每天，在我起床之前，他就离开家了。他说，他要赶在鱼儿们醒来之前到达海湾。就出口而言，温哥华是北美最大的港口。这里几乎不会上冻，所以爸爸要一年到头辛苦地工作。

鱼是这里的主要资源。爸爸说从加拿大出口的鱼，这里占出口总量的80%。其他资源有铁矿石、镍、锌、铜、金、银、煤和油。我是在加拿大数据网上得到这些信息的（你也可以查阅一下）。

---

section *n.* 部分；节

freeze *v.* （使）冻结；结冰

export *n.* 输出；出口（物）

My mom drives my brother and me to school every day. She's a French teacher (both English and French are the official languages here) at my brother's school. He's in 12th grade, so next year he will go to college. Some of my classmates take the bus or the train to get to school, and a few ride their bikes. School starts at 8:30 and ends at 3:00.

I'm in 4th grade, like you, and my most favorite class is social studies. *Right now* we're studying the Canadian government, lucky for you! Let me give you some facts about the government from my notebook.

Canada is a democracy, a government run by the people, just like the United States, but we're a confederation, not a republic like you.

每天是妈妈开车送我和哥哥去上学。妈妈任教于哥哥所在的学校，教授法语（英语和法语都是我们这里的官方语言）。哥哥上12年级了，明年就要上大学了。我的一些同学乘公交车或火车上学，也有一些同学骑自行车。我们8点30分上课，下午3点放学。

同你一样，我才上4年级。我最喜欢的课程是社会学科。目前，我们正在学习关于加拿大政府的知识。多巧呀！让我把笔记里关于加拿大政府的一些内容说给你听听吧。

加拿大是一个民主的国家，如同美国，拥有一个民治的政府。但我们是邦联制，不像你们是共和制。我想，区别就在我们的省要比你们的州更

---

right now 目前；此时

I think the difference is that our provinces are more *independent* than your states.

We also have a constitutional monarchy in which the king or queen of England is our *chief* of state. The prime minister leads Parliament (no president here). Canada's Parliament is made up of two houses, the Senate with 104 members and the House of Commons with 301 members. Hope that helps a little.

I have to go (my mom is calling me because it's time for *lacrosse* practice). I'll try to answer the rest of your questions when I get back.

Talk to you soon,

Jacqueline

加独立吧。

我们也是君主立宪制，英国国王或女王是国家最高首领。总理领导议会（这里没有总统）。加拿大的议会由两院组成，参议院有104名成员，众议院有301名成员。希望这些信息能对你有些用。

我得走了（妈妈在叫我，我得去做曲棍球练习了）。回来后，我再继续回答你的其他问题。

稍后联系

杰奎琳

---

independent *adj.* 自主的
lacrosse *n.* 长曲棍球

chief *n.* 首领

Subject: Lacrosse?

Hi Jacqueline,

Thanks so much. What's lacrosse? Is it like *soccer*? That's what I play.

My mom was *wondering* where your grandparents are from. My grandparents are from Germany.

What do you do for fun? Every summer, my family goes to Florida and relaxes on the *beach*. Do you take any family vacations? Canada sounds so cool. Hope practice was fun.

Your friend,

Stephanie

主题：曲棍球？

杰奎琳：

你好！太感谢你的资料了。曲棍球是什么？像足球吗？我喜欢玩足球。

我妈妈很好奇你的祖父母来自哪里。我的祖父母是来自德国的。

你平时都做些什么娱乐活动？每年夏天，我们全家会去佛罗里达度假，在海滩上休闲放松。你们也会全家出去旅行吗？加拿大听起来很酷。希望你练习得开心。

你的朋友
斯蒂芬妮

---

soccer *n.* （美）足球
beach *n.* 海滩；海滨

wonder *v.* 想知道；对……好奇

Subject: Family *heritage*, family vacation

Hi Stephanie,

Practice was *tough*, I'm pretty tired, but I think I'm even more hungry. My mom is upstairs cooking dinner—we're having caribou. She learned how to make it from my grandpa who was Inuit. Looks like I'm starting to answer your family heritage questions.

Before I do that, I should tell you that, yes, I do play soccer but only in gym class, and it's not as fun as lacrosse. Lacrosse is kind of like soccer, but we use sticks with baskets on the end to pass the ball to another player or hopefully into a goal that's much smaller than a soccer goal.

Okay, back to my family. My dad's *ancestors* are from England. He

主题：家庭传统，家庭度假
斯蒂芬妮：

你好！训练很艰苦，我感觉很累，但是现在更想吃些东西。妈妈上楼去做饭了——我们要吃驯鹿肉了。妈妈从外公那里学会烹饪驯鹿的，外公是因纽特人。看来我要开始回答你关于家庭传统的问题了。

在回答这些问题前，我得说明，我确实踢足球，但只是在体育课上。而且我觉得它没有曲棍球有意思。曲棍球有点像足球，但是我们要使用一端系着网篮的长棍来传球，或者把球投进一个比足球球门要小很多的球门里。

好了，说回我的家庭吧。我爸爸的祖先来自英国。可以追根溯源到

heritage *n.* 传统；文化遗产
ancestor *n.* 祖宗；祖先

tough *adj.* 艰苦的；困难的

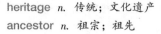

can trace them as far back as the Klondike Gold Rush of 1897! My mother's father was Inuit, like I said, but her mother was of French *descent* — and that's why she knows French so well. To answer your religion question, most Canadians are Roman Catholic. Many others are *Protestant*, like us, or another Christian religion. Only a small number of people are Muslim, Jewish, Buddhist, or Hindu.

Yes, we take family vacations. This past summer we went to Mount Logan in the Yukon's Kluane National Park. The mountain rises to 5,959 meters (19,551 feet to you), which makes it the highest point in Canada. I was hoping that we would travel all the way across the country, all 9,984,670 square miles, but my mom and dad said that was too far. Did you know that Canada is the second

1897年的克朗代克淘金热时期。我说过外公是因纽特人，但是外婆有着法国血统——所以她很精通法语。再来谈谈宗教吧。大多数加拿大人是罗马天主教徒。像我们一样，也有一些人信奉新教。此外，则是基督教徒。只有非常小的一部分人信奉穆斯林教、犹太教、佛教或印度教。

是的，我们也有家庭度假。刚刚过去的这个夏天，我们全家去了育空克鲁恩国家公园里的洛根山。这座山高达5 959米（19 551英尺），是加拿大境内的最高峰。我希望我们能够游遍整个国家，共9 984 670平方英

---

descent *n.* 血统   Protestant *n.* 新教教徒

largest country in the world?

Canada has eight land *regions*: the Canadian Shield, the Hudson Bay Lowlands, the Western Cordillera, the Interior Lowlands, the Great Lakes-St. Lawrence Lowlands, the Appalachians, the Arctic Lowlands, and the Innuitians. Since we headed straight north from Vancouver, we stayed in the Western Cordillera land region. The *scenery* in this region is amazing. There are so many mountains (I hope this is helping your "physical geography" section).

Western Cordillera   Canadian Shield   Innuition

Interior Lowlands   Hudson Bay Lowlands Appalachian

Arctic Lowlands   Great Lakes

里。但是爸爸妈妈说这真的是很难。你知道吗？加拿大是世界上第二大的国家。

加拿大从地域上可以分成8个区：加拿大地盾，哈德逊湾低地，西科迪勒拉山，内陆低地，大湖区——圣劳伦斯低地，阿巴拉契亚山脉，北极低地和因纽特区。我们所处的温哥华在正北，属于西科迪勒拉山地区。这里的风光美极了。这里有许多山脉（希望这些对"自然地理"部分有帮助）。

第一行从左至右分别为：西科迪勒拉山区、加拿大地盾区、因纽特区

第二行从左至右分别为：内陆低地区、哈德逊湾低地区、阿巴拉契亚山脉区

第三行从左至右分别为：北极低地区、大湖区

---

region *n.* 地区；地域   scenery *n.* 风景；景色；风光

The two regions I really want to see sometime in my life are the Canadian Shield and the Great Lakes-St. Lawrence Lowlands. The Canadian Shield is the largest land region in Canada—it covers about half of the country! There are *plains*, mountains, and many ancient rocks there. The Great Lakes-St. Lawrence Lowlands is mostly *rolling* lowlands. This is where Niagara Falls and Canada's main river, the St. Lawrence Seaway, are *located*. This area is often called Canada's heartland because it is a center for agricultural production and industry (Isn't that kind of like Omaha?).

Dinner's ready, so I have to run (it smells great). As soon as I'm done, I'll finish answering the rest of your questions. Here I come,

---

　　我最想去的地方是加拿大地盾区和大湖区——圣劳伦斯低地区。加拿大地盾区是加拿大最大的陆地区——它占据了加拿大国土的一半。那里有许多平原，高山和古老的岩石。大湖区——圣劳伦斯低地区几乎都是起伏的低地。尼加拉瓜瀑布和加拿大主要河流——圣劳伦斯河就位于那里。这里也通常被称作加拿大的心脏地区，因为它是农业生产中心和工业中心（是不是有点像奥马哈？）。

　　晚饭好了，我早就等不及了（闻起来太香了）。晚饭后，我会回答你

---

plain *n.* 平原；平地　　　　　　　　　rolling *adj.* 波动的；起伏的
locate *v.* 位于

caribou stew!

Jacqueline

Subject: Caribou or Moose?

Hi Jacqueline,

I had no idea Canada was so big, and I've never heard of caribou. Online, they look like moose. Is that true?

We have lots of deer here. Sometimes my friends and I see them in our *backyards*.

What are your friends like? Talk with you soon.

Your friend,

Stephanie

的其他问题。我来了，美味的炖驯鹿！

杰奎琳

主题：驯鹿还是麋鹿？

杰奎琳：

你好！我没从想过加拿大有这么大，也从没听过驯鹿。在网上看，他们很像麋鹿，对吗？

我们这里有很多鹿。有时，我和朋友们在后院就可以看到。

你的朋友们都是什么样呢？稍后联系！

你的朋友
斯蒂芬妮

---

backyard *n.* 后院

Subject: Come visit!

Hi Stephanie,

Many of my friends are on the lacrosse team but my best friend Li is not. He's from China. Did you know that a lot of people *immigrate* to Canada from Asian countries? Each year when school starts, I look around my classroom and see more kids who are Asian. I worked on an immigration *graph* with Li in Math class last year that showed the number of people who came to Canada in 2003. I am sending you a copy of the graph we made (my mom helped me *scan* it to the computer). If you can't open it, please let me know.

You know what? I just looked at your *original* list of things your teacher wanted for this report, and I think we talked about all of

---

主题：欢迎参观！

斯蒂芬妮：

你好！我的许多朋友都是曲棍球队的，但我最要好的朋友李不是，他来自中国。你知道吗？加拿大的许多移民来自亚洲国家。每年开学，我都会发现班级里又多了几个亚洲裔同学。去年的数学课上，我和李共同完成了一个关于移民的图表，用来显示在2003年移入加拿大的人口数量。我给你复制了一份（是妈妈帮忙扫描进电脑的）。如果无法打开，及时告诉我。

你知道吗？我刚刚又看了一下你报告里你们教师所需要的原始列表，

---

immigrate *v.* （外国）移居
scan *v.* 扫描

graph *n.* 图；图表；曲线图
original *adj.* 起初的；最初的

them, except for history. I'll go *bug* my dad for that (he's a big history *buff*). Here, he just scanned me a timeline from one of his history books. I'll attach it too.

9,000 B.C. Artifacts show that native Canadians are living in the present-day Ontario area.

A.D. 986 The first European, a Viking named Bjarni Herjolfsson, sees the Labrador coastline.

1608 Samuel de Champlain ("Father of New France") founds Quebec City, which is the first *permanent* English settlement in Canada.

1610 Henry Hudson *explores* Hudson Bay.

我想除了历史，其他方面我们都谈过了。这个我要请教我的父亲了（他是一个超级历史迷）。现在他正在把一本他历史书上的历史事件时间线扫描到电脑里。我随后发附件给你。

公元前9000年　历史文物显示土著加拿大人当时就生活在如今的安大略省。

公元986年　第一个欧洲人，一个叫雅尼·何尔约夫森的北欧海盗，发现了拉布拉多半岛。

1608年　萨缪尔·德·尚普兰（"新法兰西之父"）建立了魁北克城，这是英国人在加拿大建立的第一个永久居住点。

1610年　亨利·哈德逊来到哈德逊湾探险。

---

bug *v.* 骚扰；烦恼

permanent *adj.* 永久的；永恒的

buff *n.* 爱好者

explore *v.* 在……探险；考察

1702 The French and British battle in Queen Anne's War.

1818 The Canada–U.S. border is *established* at the 49th parallel.

1841 An Act of Union brings together Upper and Lower Canada, creating the Province of Canada.

1867 Sir John A. Macdonald is the first Prime Minister of the Dominion of Canada.

1897 The gold rush begins in the Yukon.

1931 Great Britain gives Canada full authority over *legislative* matters.

1965 Canada *issues* a new flag.

1989 The Canada–U.S. Free Trade Agreement starts.

1702年 英法之间爆发了"安妮女王之战"。

1818年 加拿大和美国划定了49°纬度线。

1841年 《联合议案》将上加拿大和下加拿大联合起来，建立了加拿大省。

1867年 约翰·麦克唐纳德先生成为加拿大的第一任总理。

1897年 育空区的淘金热兴起。

1931年 英国赋予加拿大立法事务的绝对权力。

1965年 加拿大颁布了新的国旗。

1989年 加美自由贸易协定开始实施。

---

establish *v.* 建立；创立；设立

issue *v.* 发行；发布

legislative *adj.* 立法的；有关立法的

1999   The Inuit Territory of Nunavut is created.

Hope I helped you with your report. Maybe this next summer, you could *persuade* your family to come visit Canada *instead of* Florida. You could visit Ottawa (the national capital) or Toronto (the largest city), but let's face it, Vancouver is the prettiest place to be in the summer. You'd love it. Can't wait to hear about Omaha and the United States next month. Take care.

Your friend,

Jacqueline

1999年   建立努纳维特因纽特人领地。

希望提供的资料对你的报告有所帮助。也许，明年夏天，你能说服你的家人来加拿大而不是佛罗里达度假。可以来看看渥太华（加拿大的首都）或多伦多（最大的城市）。但是毋庸置疑，温哥华是夏天里最美的城市。你一定会喜欢上它的。我已经迫不及待地想听听你下个月对奥哈马和美国的介绍了。保重！

你的朋友

杰奎琳

---

persuade *v.* 劝说；说服   instead of （用）……代替……

6

Australia

Introduction

The official name of Australia is The Commonwealth of Australia, but Australians call their land "Oz". It is a place so *unique*, it might have come from a fantasy story rather than real life. Many of the things you see in Australia, from the *incredible* landscapes to the amazing *creatures*, are unlike anything else on Earth. Australia has a rich and *fascinating* history. A group of people

---

澳大利亚

简介

澳大利亚的官方名字是"澳大利亚联邦",但澳大利亚人把自己的国家昵称为"Oz"(音:奥兹)。这块土地非常独特,它似乎来自于神话故事,而非现实生活。你在澳大利亚所见到的,无论是无与伦比的美景,还是令人惊叹的生物,都与其他地方大有差别。澳大利亚有着丰富迷人的历史。当地的土著人已经在澳大利亚生活了40 000多年。在

---

unique *adj.* 唯一的;独一无二的
creature *n.* 生物;动物

incredible *adj.* 妙极的;了不起的
fascinating *adj.* 迷人的;让人着迷的

called Aborigines has lived in Australia for over 40,000 years. Britain *claimed* Australia just over 200 years ago. Since then, the country has changed from a small colony to a nation with *approximately* 20 million citizens.

Australia's population is also unique. Although Australia has lots of industry, most areas have almost no people. Those under-populated areas are known as the Outback, and the people who live there have a *frontier* spirit, even in this day. However, most Australians live in cities and lead modern lives.

To learn more about the fascinating country called Australia, simply turn the page. Welcome to Australia!

200多年前，英国在澳大利亚建立了殖民地。自此，澳大利亚从一个小殖民地发展成为一个有着2 000万国民的国家。

澳大利亚的人口也很独特。尽管澳大利亚有很多行业，但是很多地区几乎是无人区。人口稀少的地区被称作"内地"，住在那里的人都有种拓荒精神，即使今天也是一样。但是，大多数澳大利亚人还是住在城市里，过着现代人的生活。

要了解更多有关澳大利亚的精彩，翻到下一页就可以了。欢迎来到澳大利亚！

---

claim *v.* 声称；断言
frontier *adj.* 开拓的

approximately *adv.* 大约；大概

Geography

Australia is the only country that is also a *continent* (landmass). Australia is the oldest continent, at 40 million years old, the smallest continent, and the world's largest island! It is also the world's flattest continent. Australia is the sixth largest country in the world. It is as large as the United States (not counting Hawaii and Alaska). The continent covers 7,772,535 square kilometers (3,842,674 sq mi.) of land.

Australia is located in the southern *hemisphere* (half of the earth). The Indian Ocean borders Australia on the west and south, while the Pacific Ocean surrounds the northern and eastern edges. The country of Australia includes the island state of Tasmania, which is 240 kilometers (150 mi.) off Australia's southern *tip*, across the Bass

---

地理条件

澳大利亚是唯一一个独占一个洲（大陆）的国家。澳大利亚是地球上最古老的大陆，有4 000万年的历史，它是世界上面积最小的大陆，同时又是世界上最大的岛屿！它也是世界上地势最平坦的大陆。澳大利亚是世界第六大国。它的面积同美国（夏威夷和阿拉斯加不计在内）的面积一样大，达7 772 535平方公里（合3 842 674平方英里）。

澳大利亚位于南半球（半球指地球的一半）。其国境西南邻近印度洋，东北被太平洋环绕。澳大利亚国土还包括塔斯马尼亚岛，此岛位于澳大利亚大陆以南240公里（合150英里），横穿巴斯海峡。

---

continent *n.* 大陆；洲　　　　　　　　hemisphere *n.* （地球的）半球

tip *n.* 末梢；尖端；顶端

Strait.

There are three main areas in Australia: the Western Plateau, the Central Lowlands, and the Eastern Highlands. The Western Plateau, covering two-thirds of Australia, is a flat, dry, desert area with hot weather. Scientists have found the world's oldest rocks in the Western Plateau. Dry grasslands are found in the Central Lowlands, where it is hot all year during the day, but can be very cold at night. The Great Dividing Range, part of the Eastern Highlands, holds rivers, *valleys*, and Australia's highest mountains.

Kangaroos, crocodiles, koala bears, Tasmanian devils, cockatoos, and frilled lizards have become symbols of Australia.

在澳大利亚有三个主要区域：西部高原、中部平原和东部山地。西部高原约占澳大利亚面积的2/3，那里是地势平坦、气候干燥、终年高温的沙漠地区。科学家们已经在西部高原发现了世界上最古老的岩石。中部平原则是终年白天炎热，但夜间温度可能降到极低的多干旱草原，大分水岭山脉——上有众多河流、峡谷，以及澳大利亚最高的山脉，位于东部山地地区。

袋鼠、鳄鱼、考拉熊、袋獾、美冠鹦鹉、皱褶蜥蜴，这些动物都成了澳大利亚的象征。

---

valley *n.* 山谷

Animals

Australia's animals are amazing! Because of the continent's *isolation* and harsh conditions, animals seen nowhere else on Earth have developed.

Today, some of these animals are *threatened* (in danger of dying out and becoming extinct). As cities grow larger, the natural areas have grown smaller. Homes and food for some animals are becoming *scarce*.

Only in Australia can you find a platypus. This unusual animal has four legs, fur, beady eyes, a tail like a beaver's, a duck's bill, and webbed feet. When a British scientist first saw a platypus, he believed someone was playing a practical joke! An adult male

动物

澳大利亚的动物令人叫绝！由于这块大陆孤立、恶劣的生存条件，在地球上其他地方见不到的动物在这里却生活得如鱼得水。

在今天，有些动物的生存已经受到威胁（正在消失或濒临灭绝）。城市规模越来越大，自然区域就越来越小。一些动物的家园和食物都日趋稀少。

只有在澳大利亚，你才能看到鸭嘴兽。这种奇怪的动物有四条腿，有皮毛，豆子一样的眼睛，河狸一样的尾巴，鸭子一样的嘴巴，还有带蹼的脚掌。一个英国科学家第一次看见鸭嘴兽的时候，以为有人在搞恶作剧呢！一只成年雄性鸭嘴兽能够从踝部射出毒药。尽管鸭嘴兽属于哺乳动物

isolation *n.* 隔离；孤寂
scarce *adj.* 缺乏的；不足的

threaten *v.* 威胁

platypus can shoot poison from its ankle. Although a platypus is a mammal (a warm-blooded animal that nurses its young), females lay eggs.

There are around 700 types of Australian snakes and lizards. When one lizard called a thorny devil feels threatened, it *inflates* with air to look bigger and shows its skin spikes. If it's really *scared*, it *tucks* its head between its front legs.

Koalas look like teddy bears, but they aren't bears at all. They're actually related to the kangaroo, another common Australian animal. Koalas are the only animals besides primates (a group of

---

（即一种恒温、哺育后代的动物），但雌性鸭嘴兽仍然会产蛋。

澳大利亚的蛇与蜥蜴有700种之多。有种叫作棘蜥的蜥蜴如果感觉到危险，就会充气膨胀起来看着更高大，显露出皮肤上的长刺。如果它实在很怕，就会把头夹在前腿之间。

考拉看起来像是泰迪熊，但它们根本不是熊。它们实际上和澳大利亚非常常见的另外一种动物——袋鼠——有着紧密的联系。除了灵长类动物（即包括人、猿猴和猴子在内的这类动物）之外，考拉是唯一有独特指纹

---

inflate *v.* （使）充分；长大　　　　scared *adj.* 惊恐的；恐惧的
tuck *v.* 把……塞入；藏入

animals that includes humans, apes, and monkeys) that have unique fingerprints.

The platypus, thorny devil, and the koala are just three of a large number of animals found only in Australia!

Most of Australia's mammals are *marsupials*. A marsupial gives birth to a tiny, helpless baby that lives in a pouch or pocket on its mother's body. On other continents, most marsupials disappeared long ago. But Australia's isolation allowed marsupials to *thrive*. Kangaroos, wallabies, and koalas are all marsupials.

The animals on these pages are just a few of the large number of creatures found only in Australia!

的动物。

鸭嘴兽、棘蜥和考拉只是澳大利亚独有的众多动物种类中的三种而已！

澳大利亚的哺乳动物大多是有袋动物。有袋动物将不能独立生活的幼仔放在妈妈腹袋或口袋里。在其他大陆，有袋动物很久以前就灭绝了。但澳大利亚的隔绝使得有袋动物可以在这里繁衍生息。袋鼠、小袋鼠和考拉都属于有袋动物。

这里所列的动物只是在澳大利亚发现的众多动物种类中的几种而已！

---

marsupial *n.* 有袋动物　　　　　　　　　　thrive *v.* 欣欣向荣；茁壮成长

The Outback

The Australian Outback is the huge dry inland area. Rain may not fall there for years at a time. There can be hundreds of miles between "towns", which are usually just a few buildings. The Outback has *enormous* deserts—the world's largest desert areas outside the Sahara. There are also some mountainous regions.

There are many colorfully *gorgeous* sights here: enormous golden plains, red rocks, and purple mountain ranges. The landscape is empty and stretches forever. This is truly frontier country for hardy

---

内地

澳大利亚的内地是大面积的干旱内陆地区。有时几年都不下一场雨。在"城镇"之间可能隔有几百英里的距离，所谓的"城镇"通常只是几幢楼而已。内地有着广袤的沙漠——除了撒哈拉沙漠以外的世界最大沙漠。内地也有部分山区。

在内地，有着许多引人入胜的景观：广阔的金色平原、红色的岩石和紫色的山脉。放眼望去，绵延不绝。这里真正是吃苦耐劳的先锋者们拓荒的地方。

---

enormous *adj.* 巨大的；庞大的　　　　gorgeous *adj.* 美丽动人的；引人入胜的

pioneers.

If you visit the Outback, keep your eye out for wild camels! The animals were brought here in the 1870s as desert *transportation*. Today, the only wild camels in the world live in the Outback. Some tourist places offer camel tours to visitors.

Some residents of the Outback live and work on enormous *ranches* called "stations". Some stations are actually larger than some small countries! Other people work in mining and in oil production. The only city in the outback, Alice Springs, welcomes tourists who come to visit Uluru.

　　如果你到了内地，一定要小心野骆驼！它们是19世纪70年代被带到沙漠里当运输工具的。现在，世界上只有在澳大利亚内地才能见到野骆驼。有些旅游机构会向参观者们提供骆驼旅行。

　　在内地的居民生活和工作都在宽广的牧场里，他们把牧场叫作"站"。实际上，有些"站"比小的国家还要大一些！其他人在煤矿或油田工作。内地的唯一一个城市是艾利斯斯普林斯，欢迎所有来参观乌卢鲁巨岩的游客们到此光临。

---

transportation　*n.*　交通工具；运输工具　　　　　　ranch　*n.*　大牧场；大农场

Do You Know?

The Great Barrier Reef, off the coast of Australia, is the largest coral reef system in the world. It is home to more than 2,000 types of fish, many types of coral, and other sea creatures, sea plants, and birds. Just how big is the Great Barrier Reef? You can actually see it from space!

Do You Know?

Aborigines used boomerangs in games, to hunt and fight, and to build fires by *rubbing* the edges against other sticks. The word "boomerang" simply means "throwing stick". Not all boomerangs were meant to come back to the thrower. By 8,000 BC, the Aborigines invented a "returning boomerang" that would *swirl* in the air and return to the thrower.

你知道吗?
远离澳大利亚海岸的大堡礁是世界最大的珊瑚礁群。2 000多种鱼类、多种珊瑚和其他的海洋动物，海洋植物以及鸟类都以此为家。大堡礁到底有多大？大到你在太空都能看得见！

你知道吗?
土著居民用回力刀进行捕猎和比赛，还可以用来钻木取火。英文中"回力刀"一词其实就是"扔木棍"。并不是所有的木棍都会回到投掷者这里来的。到公元前8000年，土著居民发明了一种"回旋飞刀"，这种刀可以在空中飞旋后回到投掷者手里。

rub v. 摩擦　　　　　　　　　　swirl v. 旋转；打旋

History

The first people living in Australia were the Aborigines. They probably traveled by sea from Asia more than 40,000 years ago. By the time Europeans settled Australia, there may have been close to one million Aborigines in Australia. The early Aborigines were nomads (people who moved *frequently*). They hunted and gathered food in small groups and lived in *temporary* mud homes. They had at least 300 different languages.

In the 17th century, Dutch, Portuguese, and Spanish sailors viewed Australia from their ships. The Dutch landed in 1606 and explored for around 150 years, but decided the land was *worthless*. In 1688, the first Englishman, William Dampier, arrived. Although

---

历史

最早住在澳大利亚的人是土著居民。他们可能是40 000年以前从亚洲通过海路来到这里的。到欧洲人在澳大利亚定居时,在澳洲的土著居民已经接近100万了。早期的土著居民是游牧民(他们经常搬迁、居无定所)。他们几个人一起捕猎、收集食物,住在临时的泥屋里。他们讲的语言至少有300种。

17世纪时,荷兰、葡萄牙和西班牙的航海家们从船上看到澳大利亚。荷兰人1606年在澳大利亚登陆,探索了大约150年,结论是这片土地一文不值。1688年,威廉·丹皮尔成了第一个到达澳大利亚的英国人。

---

frequently *adv.* 频繁地;屡次地

worthless *adj.* 无价值的;没用处的

temporary *adj.* 临时的;暂时的

Dampier wasn't *impressed* with Australia, he wrote a book about what he saw.

Finally, in 1770, an Englishman, Captain James Cook, arrived in Australia. He claimed Australia's east coast for Britain, calling it New South Wales. Because of *crowding* in British prisons, England established a *convict* colony (a settlement of prisoners) in Australia. The first settlement had 759 prisoners (568 men and 191 women), 200 soldiers, and 40 wives and children of the soldiers. These people lived in tents and ate native animals and food sent from England.

When that first settlement survived, more settlers began to arrive. Free settlers *set up* farms, explored the land, and searched for minerals. By the early 1800s, explorers had sailed around Australia

---

尽管澳大利亚并没给丹皮尔留下很深的印象，他还是写了一本书，记录了他所见到的一切。

终于在1770年，又一个英国人——船长詹姆斯·库克——到达了澳大利亚。他宣称澳大利亚的东海岸为英国所有，称这里为"新南威尔士"。因为英国的监狱犯人过多，所以英格兰在澳大利亚建立了一个安置罪犯的殖民地。最早住在这里的一批犯人有759人（其中男犯568人，女犯191人），士兵200人、士兵配偶40人还有他们的孩子。这些人住在帐篷里，以当地的动物为食，也吃从英格兰运送来的食物。

当最早的定居者生存下来之后，就有更多的人来此定居。自由的定居

---

impress *v.* 使留下印象
convict *n.* 囚犯

crowding *n.* 人群
set up 创建；建立

and traveled through the interior. Different colonies (groups from *distant* lands, still tied to the parent country) settled throughout the continent during the 19th century.

Do You Know?

Six colonies were established by free settlers and former convicts during the 1700s and 1800s.

The Aborigines did not farewell after Britain began colonizing Australia. Many died *due to* new diseases brought into the country. Others died because of fighting between the newcomers and the

者建起农场、开发土地，寻找矿物资源。到19世纪早期，探险者们已经在澳大利亚外围环游过，他们开始在澳大利亚内陆进行探索了。19世纪，整个大陆被划分成了不同的殖民地（即远离殖民国地盘，但仍隶属于殖民国管辖的土地）。

你知道吗？

在18到19世纪之间，自由的定居者和早期的罪犯建立了六个殖民地。

在英国人将澳大利亚设为殖民地之后，土著人并没有离开那里。但是

---

distant *adj.* 遥远的；远距离的 　　　　　　　　　　due to　由于

Aboriginal people. In the 1850s, the British forced many of the surviving natives to live on reservations.

Gold was discovered in New South Wales and in Victoria in 1851. In the gold rush that followed, men from all over Australia, as well as European and Chinese immigrants, *rushed to* the gold fields. Some found gold and became wealthy, while others did not.

The colonies became states. In 1901, they united under one government and called themselves the Commonwealth of Australia. Britain entered World War I in 1914, with Australia fighting *alongside*.

A huge depression (a period of poverty) struck Australia in 1929.

许多人因为外来的新型疾病而丧命。还有人死于与外来者发生的争斗中。19世纪50年代，英国人强迫许多活下来的当地人到保留地上去生活。

1851年人们在新南威尔士和维多利亚发现了黄金。之后就出现了"淘金热"，来自澳大利亚本国的人，还有来自欧洲和中国的移民都蜂拥到发现金矿的地方。有些人淘到了黄金，摇身变成有钱人，同样的有些人则没能找到。

殖民地逐渐变成各个州。1901年，各州团结在一个政府下，称其为"澳大利亚联邦"。英国在1914年参加第一次世界大战，澳大利亚与其并肩作战。

1929年，澳大利亚经历了经济大萧条（一段贫困期）。到1931年，

---

rush to 奔；奔赴　　　　　alongside *adv.* 与……一起

By 1931, one out of every three workers was unemployed, and many were homeless. Business and the economy improved from 1934 to 1937. During World War II, Australians fought alongside Allied soldiers.

Early Australian immigration (people moving into a country) laws had allowed mostly northern Europeans to enter the country. This changed in the 1960s and 1970s, allowing more Asian immigrants.

In 1967, voters chose to include Aborigines as citizens in all the states for the first time. Some land rights were given to Aboriginal citizens in 1972. Aborigines, Australia's poorest group, struggle to *maintain* their rights even today.

1/3的工人失业，还有许多人无家可归。1934至1937年间，商业与经济逐步好转。在第二次世界大战期间，澳大利亚人仍与联军并肩作战。

　　早期澳大利亚的移民法（移民指搬到另一个国家去住的人）允许大多数北欧人移居至此。这种情况在1960至1970年间有所改变，澳大利亚开始接受更多来自亚洲的移民。

　　1967年，选举者们首次在各州将土著人认定为国家公民。1972年土著人获得了一些地方性的权利。但直到今天，土著人，这个澳大利亚最贫困的群体，仍然在为保留自己的权利而斗争。

---

maintain *v.* 保持或维持某事物

Modern Australia

Australia is a democracy, with three levels of government: local, state, and federal. The country's leader, who is chosen by elected lawmakers, is called the Prime Minister. Australians speak English, and they pay for purchases with Australian dollars. Much of Australian culture comes from Britain. Australians still honor the queen of Britain as their *ceremonial* head of state. In 1999, Australians voted to keep this *loyalty* to Britain.

In 2003, approximately 20 million people lived in Australia. Of all Australians, about 92 percent are Caucasian, or white, and 7 percent are Asian. Today, 350,000 Aboriginal people live in Australia. Almost

---

现代澳大利亚

澳大利亚是个民主国家，有三级政府：地方政府、州政府和联邦政府。国家领导人是总理，由立法者选出。澳大利亚人讲英语，通用货币是澳元。澳大利亚文化大部分是受了英国的影响。澳大利亚人名义上的国家元首仍然是英国女王。1999年，澳大利亚人投票通过继续保持对英国效忠。

2003年，澳大利亚常住人口大约有2 000万。在所有澳大利亚人中，大约92%为高加索人或称白人，7%为亚洲人。目前，在澳大利亚有35万土著居民。几乎每一个成年澳大利亚人都识字！

---

ceremonial *adj.* 仪式的；礼节的　　　　　　　　loyalty *n.* 忠诚；忠心

every single Australian adult can read!

About 90 percent of Australians live in cities. Australian cities are modern, but they are long distances from each other.

Australia's capital city is Canberra, which is within New South Wales. Although it is the center of politics and government, it has some small-town *charms*. There are only around 500,000 residents. The city has art *museums*, the High Court of Australia, the Australian National University, and other important places.

Sydney is Australia's largest city, with a population above 4 million. Within the city lie a business *district*, Chinatown, The Botanic Gardens, museums and art *galleries*, and many old buildings. Surrounding the city are national parks filled with plants and animals. Sydney is also home to some of the most beautiful beaches in the

---

大约有90%的澳大利亚人住在城市里。澳大利亚的城市非常现代，但是城市之间相距遥远。

澳大利亚的首都是堪培拉，地处新南威尔士州。尽管这里是政治中心和政府所在地，它仍然散发着一些小城镇的魅力。市内只有大概50万居民。这里有艺术博物馆、澳大利亚高级法院、澳大利亚国立大学和一些其他的重要场所。

悉尼是澳大利亚最大的城市，有超出400万人口。在悉尼，有一个商业区、有唐人街、有皇家植物园、有多所博物馆和艺术展馆，还有很多古老的建筑。在城市周围，有满是动植物的国家公园。悉尼也有着世界上最

---

charm *n.* 魅力；吸引力
district *n.* 地区；区域

museum *n.* 博物馆
gallery *n.* 画廊；走廊

world.

Australia's other big cities include Melbourne, Brisbane, Perth, and Adelaide. Like almost all of Australia's cities, these are right along the coast.

While Australia has little farmland, it is rich in minerals and *precious* gems.

At one time, the wool industry was Australia's largest business, but that is no longer the case. Major Australian industries include mining, the *manufacture* of industrial and transportation equipment, construction, food processing, chemicals, and steel. Some new industries are winemaking and *tourism*.

The country's natural resources include bauxite (a claylike material from which aluminum is obtained), coal, iron ore, copper, tin, silver, uranium, nickel, natural gas, and petroleum. Australia also

---

美丽的几处海滩。

　　澳大利亚其他较大的城市有墨尔本、布里斯班、佩斯和阿德莱得。与几乎所有的澳大利亚城市一样，这些城市也都地处海边。

　　澳大利亚几乎没有农田，但是有丰富的矿产和珍贵的宝石。

　　有段时间，羊毛业是澳大利亚最大的行业，但现在情况不同了。澳大利亚的主要工业包括矿业、工业与运输设备的加工业、建筑业、食品加工业、化学药物和钢铁生产。还有些新兴的行业包括制酒业和旅游业。

　　澳大利亚的自然资源包括铝土岩（一种产铝的粘土状物质）、煤、铁矿石、铜、锡、银、铀、镍、天然气和石油。澳大利亚也出口肉类、羊

---

precious *adj.* 宝贵的；珍贵的　　　　manufacture *n.* 制造；生产
tourism *n.* 旅游业

exports meat, wool, wheat, sugar, and machinery. Australia is the world's largest producer of diamonds.

Explore More

1. At the Library

Ask your school or local librarian to help you find information about Australia. You can *look up* books on Australian history, the Outback, Aborigines, and modern Australia. You can also find many books on unusual Australian animals, such as kangaroos, wallabies, and koalas.

2. On the Internet

A. In the address window, type www.google.com.

B. Pick a subject you'd like to explore, such as the Outback, and

---

毛、小麦、糖和器械。澳大利亚还是世界上最大的钻石产地。

继续探索

1.在图书馆

可以让你学校或当地的图书管理员帮你找找关于澳大利亚的信息。你可以在书里查阅澳大利亚的历史、内地、土著人和现代澳洲近况。你也会在很多书里看到澳大利亚独有的动物，比如说袋鼠、小袋鼠和考拉等等。

2.在上网

A. 在地址栏，输入www.google.com。

B. 选择一个你想了解的主题，比如说"内地"，就把关键词输入搜

---

look up 查检（事实或信息）

type it in the search window. Click on "Google Search".

C. Read the colored links. Click on one that looks interesting.

D. If you want to explore more links, click on the "Back" arrow on the top left.

E. Try searching for other subjects, such as kangaroos, Aborigines, Sydney, or other topics.

3. In the Media

Australia produces a diverse selection of movies, music, art, and *theater*. Ask your teacher, parent, or librarian to help you find films that take place in Australia or music that comes from Australia. You might be surprised by the richness of Australia's landscape and modern culture.

索栏里。点击"搜索"。

C. 阅读高亮的链接。点击你觉得有趣的链接。

D. 如果你想得到更多链接，点击左上角的"返回"箭头。

E. 试着搜索一下其他的主题，比如"袋鼠"、"土著人"、"悉尼"或其他主题。

3. 通过媒体

澳大利亚出品了大量的电影、音乐、艺术和戏剧。问问你的老师、父母，或让图书管理员帮你找一些在澳大利亚拍摄的电影或来自澳大利亚的音乐。你可能会被澳大利亚富饶的景色和现代的文化所震惊。

---

theater *n.* 戏剧

Pyramids

Introduction

The country of Egypt sits at the northeastern corner of the African continent. It was once home to the ancient Egyptian civilization. Ancient Egypt was one of the most *fascinating* cultures ever to exist. Thousands of years ago, these people studied and practiced agriculture, irrigation, architecture, engineering, and much

---

金字塔

简介

埃及位于非洲大陆的东北角。这里曾经是古埃及文明的所在。曾经孕育了世界上最神奇的文化之一。几千年以前，这里的人们就学习并实践着农业、灌溉、建筑、工程，还有很多其他的事物，边学习边付诸实践。他们建造了很多伟大的建筑，其中一项就是金字塔。了解这

---

fascinating *adj.* 吸引人的；迷人的

more. They built great structures, including the pyramids. Learning about these pyramids can help us learn a great deal about this amazing civilization.

Ancient Egypt

Egyptians began to settle along the banks of the Nile River about seven thousand years ago. At first they lived in villages, but over time the villages formed into larger groups and eventually became *tribes*. By about 3200 B.C., these tribes were united under one king, who was called the pharaoh.

The culture of ancient Egypt was dependent on the life-giving Nile River. It *provided* them with fish and birds to eat, as well as water to *irrigate* their crops. It also served as a waterway for boats, both for travel and to transport goods.

些金字塔可以让我们更多地了解这个神奇的文明。

古埃及

古埃及人大约7 000年前在尼罗河岸定居下来。他们最初住在村庄里，随着时间推移，各个村庄规模不断扩大，最终发展成了多个部落。到公元前3200年，这些部落被一位国王统一了起来。这位国王被称作法老。

古埃及的文化与其母亲河——尼罗河紧密相连。尼罗河为古埃及人提供了可食用的鱼类和鸟类，还供给了人们灌溉庄稼的水源。尼罗河也是供船只通行的水路，既可以旅游，也可以运送货物。

---

tribe *n.* 部落
irrigate *v.* 灌溉（田地或作物）

provide *v.* 向某人提供某事物

The Nile has been a busy waterway for thousands of years.

The ancient Egyptians believed in life after death. They believed that their next life would be similar to their present life and that they would need the same kinds of tools and objects in their next life. Therefore, many people were buried with a *collection* of some of the things they possessed in their *current* life. Of all the people living in ancient Egypt, no one was given a more *lavish* burial than a pharaoh.

According to the beliefs of the ancient Egyptians, the pharaoh was the son of the sun god, Re. While he was alive on Earth, the pharaoh was known as Horus. After he died, he was united with Re. The new pharaoh, who *replaced* the dead pharaoh, became the new Horus.

数千年来，尼罗河一直是一条繁忙的水路。

古埃及人相信人死后有来生。他们相信他们的来生会与今生很相似，来生也会需要现在生活所需的各种工具和物品。因此，许多人在入葬时，都同时埋葬了他们活着时所用的物品。所有生活在古埃及的人中，法老的葬礼是最铺张的。

在古埃及人的信仰中，法老是太阳神"拉"的儿子。法老在世时，人们也称他为"何露斯"。他去世后，就与"拉"融为一体。新的法老会代替死去的法老，成为新的"何露斯"。

---

collection *n.* 成堆物品

lavish *adj.* 丰富的；大量的；铺张的

current *adj.* 现在的；现行的

replace *v.* 代替；取代

The Egyptians believed that in order for a pharaoh to live forever and continue to bless their lives, his body had to be preserved so that his spirit would stay alive. They built pyramids to honor pharaohs who had died. Each pyramid held a pharaoh's body, as well as riches and treasures meant to accompany him in the next life. The pyramid also protected the pharaoh's tomb and its treasures from theft. *In addition*, it served as a *monument* to the pharaoh's greatness.

Do You Know?

The shape of a pyramid represents the sun's rays shining on the Earth. Ancient Egyptians believed that a pharaoh who died *ascended* to heaven on the rays of the sun.

埃及人相信为了让法老永生，并且永远保佑他们，法老的遗体必须保存起来，这样他的精神才能永存。古埃及人建造了金字塔来纪念去世的法老。每一座金字塔都存放着一位法老的遗体，同时还有大量的珍宝财富，供他来生使用。金字塔也保护着法老的墓室和里面的财富，避免被盗。金字塔也是标志着法老之神圣的纪念碑。

你知道吗？

金字塔的形状代表着阳光照在地球上的样子。古埃及人相信法老去世后会沿着太阳的光线升上天堂。

---

in addition 加之；除……之外
ascend v. 上升；升高

monument n. 纪念像；纪念物

Building a Pyramid

A pharaoh planned the construction of his pyramid long before he was expected to die, since finishing it would take many years. A large pyramid could take as long as twenty years to complete. Building a pyramid *required* thousands of people. Some were skilled workers, such as architects who designed the overall structure on orders from the pharaoh. People with special knowledge were also required to *properly* remove the stone from a *quarry* and to shape the stone. After a pyramid was built, skilled sculptors and painters decorated it. A *scribe* recorded all the materials needed for building the pyramid using the ancient Egyptian writing system, called hieroglyphics. Hieroglyphics consist of a series of small pictures that represent ideas.

建造金字塔

法老在他去世以前很久就会计划他的金字塔的建造，因为建造过程要花上很多年。一座大型的金字塔要花上大约20年才能完成。建造金字塔需要上千名劳工。有一些是技术工人，比如说根据法老的命令设计整座建筑的建筑师。有着专门知识的人要到采石场选好石料，并且做好外形。金字塔建完之后，技术高超的雕刻师和画家就开始进行装饰。一名文书用古埃及的书写方式——象形文字——记录下建造金字塔所需的全部材料。象形文字是由一系列表达思想的图画构成的。

---

require *v.* 需要

quarry *n.* 采石场；石矿

properly *adv.* 适当地；恰当地

scribe *n.* （印刷术发明之前的）抄写员

Many men were needed to pull each large stone on a sledge.

In addition to these specialized *tasks*, other workers were required to move the heavy stones. They moved some stones from the quarry to the building site by boat. Other stones were put on sledges, or large wooden sleds, which were then *dragged* across the desert sands.

Until recently, historians believed that much of this difficult work was forced on laborers who served as slaves. They included prisoners and people who owed money to the pharaoh. But in 1990, a tourist traveling in Egypt *stumbled on* the remains of an ancient city where workers who helped build the pyramids of Giza were once believed to have lived. *Evidence* from the city suggests that the

---

要把一块大石头放到雪橇上，需要许多人一起完成。

除了这些专门的工作之外，其他的工人都要去搬运很重的石头。他们把一些石头用船从采石场运送到建筑地点。另外一些石头则要放在雪橇板上，或者木制的大雪橇上，然后一路拉到沙漠中去。

直到最近，历史学家们相信这种重体力劳动是强迫像奴隶一样使唤的劳工们完成的。他们包括犯人，还有欠法老钱的人。但是1990年，一位到埃及的游客意外地发现了一座古城的残骸，而这里也被认为建造吉萨金字塔的工人们曾经在这里居住过。从这座古城发现的证据表明，建造金

---

task *n.* 必须做的工作；任务
stumble on sth 意外或偶然地发现某事物

drag *v.* 拖；拉；扯
evidence *n.* 迹象；痕迹；证据

people who built those pyramids were not slaves, but rather skilled craftsmen—about 15,000 of them. Written records suggest that the workers were treated well while they worked on the pyramids.

It is believed that farmers also *participated* in the building of pyramids, especially during the flood season when they could not farm. Farmers depended on floods to deposit *fertile* soil for crops. Because the pharaoh was believed to be the son of a god, farmers thought he was able to *guarantee* good floods. They were glad to serve the pharaoh in exchange for the fertile soil brought by the floods.

Do You Know?

Each stone in the Great Pyramid weighed up to two tons. This is as much as a car weight.

字塔的并不是奴隶，而是有手艺的工匠——大约有15 000名。文字记载表明，工人们在建造金字塔期间，得到了很不错的待遇。

人们认为当时的农民们也参加了建造金字塔的工作，特别是在洪灾季节无法耕种的时候。农民们指望洪水来为庄稼孕育肥沃的土壤。因为法老被看作是神的儿子，所以农民们相信法老会保证他们有充足的洪水。他们很乐意用效忠法老来换取肥沃的土壤。

你知道吗？

大金字塔里面的每一块石头都重达2吨。这个重量甚至赶上一辆汽车了。

---

participate *v.* 参加；参与
guarantee *v.* 担保；保证

fertile *adj.* 肥沃的；富饶的

The location of a pyramid had to be *determined* very carefully. The site needed to be on rocky ground to support the *immense* weight of the finished pyramid. It needed to be near the Nile River so that some of the stones could be transported by water from the quarry to the building site. The site had to be located on the west bank of the Nile because the west was where the sun set each night and where the dead were believed to exist.

The exact position of the pyramid also needed to be determined carefully, since the sides had to face exact north, south, east, and west. An astronomer-priest was *summoned* to observe the stars in order to determine true north. During the actual building of a pyramid, many ceremonies were performed to ensure the support of the gods in the *endeavor*.

　　金字塔建造位置的选择要极其谨慎。选址处必须是坚硬的石地以此来支撑完工的金字塔的巨大重量。选址处还要临近尼罗河，这样一些石料就可以从采石场通过水路运送。同时金字塔还要地处尼罗河西岸，因为西岸是每晚日落的地方，人们相信去世的灵魂也在那里。

　　金字塔的精确方位也要谨慎地决定，因为金字塔的四个面要准确地朝向东、南、西、北。识天相的祭司会被招来观望星辰，以确定准确的北方。在金字塔建造期间，要举行许多仪式，确保工程会得到神最大的保护。

---

determine　*v.* 确定；决定
summon　*v.* 召唤某人；召集（大家）

immense　*adj.* 巨大的
endeavor　*n.* 努力；尽力

Several kinds of stone were used in the building of a pyramid. The core of the pyramid was made from local limestone. Other limestone of finer *quality*, brought from far away, was used to make the outer *shell* of the pyramid. Granite from even farther away was used for the pharaoh's coffin, called a sarcophagus, as well as to decorate the burial chamber.

After the location and position of the pyramid were decided on, the surface of the ground was leveled. After leveling the ground, the workers began the actual labor of building the pyramid.

The internal structure of a pyramid was designed to outsmart thieves and keep them from the burial chamber and its treasures. If the burial chamber was at or below ground level, it was put in place first, and then the pyramid was built around it in *horizontal* layers.

在建造金字塔期间，要用到几种石料。金字塔的中心部分使用当地的石灰石。其他的从较远地方运来的优质石灰石则用来建造金字塔的外壁。从更远处运来的花岗石被用来打造法老的棺材，称作"石棺"。这些石头也用来装饰墓室。

在建造地点和具体方位确定以后，选址处地表要打平。打平之后，工人们就真正开始了建造金字塔的工作。

金字塔的内部结构设计精妙，可以防止盗贼进入墓室或盗走财宝。如果墓室与地面平齐或低于地面，就要先建好墓室，再在墓室周围水平建起

---

quality *n.* 质量；品质   shell *n.* 外壳
horizontal *adj.* 平的；水平的

Ramps were built against the sides of the pyramid, and the huge stones were dragged up the ramps and put in position.

A series of passageways and rooms included dead ends and empty chambers to confuse anyone trying to *loot* the tomb. *Enormous* slabs of stone blocked the entrance to the real tomb.

TRY THIS!

Build a Pyramid

Using sugar cubes or cubes fashioned out of clay, build a model pyramid. You can build a pyramid with steps, a flat-sided pyramid, or one of your own design.

金字塔。金字塔的各面会建起斜坡，大块的石头要从斜坡拉上去，放到合适的位置上。

金字塔内设计有许多通道和房间用来迷惑任何想要掠夺墓室财物的人，其中也包括一些死胡同和空房间。大量的厚石板会挡住真正的墓室入口。

试一试！

建造金字塔

使用方糖块或方形泥土块，造一个金字塔模型。你可以建造一座有台阶的金字塔，一座有斜面的金字塔，或者一座你自己设计的金字塔。

---

loot *v.* 抢劫；劫掠

enormous *adj.* 巨大的；极大的

Preparing the Body

The ancient Egyptians had a special *procedure* for preparing the body of an important person for burial. This technique, called mummification, preserved the body for thousands of years. The body was taken to an embalmer, who removed the insides and preserved them in canopic jars. Each jar had a *lid* in the shape of a guardian god. The body then was left to dry for forty days. Then it was washed, rubbed with oil and fragrant *spices*, and packed with preservatives. Afterward, it was wrapped with many layers of linen soaked in resin to hold its shape. A decorative mask was placed on the head, and the entire body was placed in a coffin. Coffins were ornately painted.

处理尸体

古埃及人要为一个重要人物入葬，有一套特殊的程序来处理尸体。这种保存尸体的方式叫作"木乃伊化"，可以将尸体保存上千年。尸体先被带到一个尸体防腐者那里，他会去除尸体脏腑，并将脏腑保存在克诺珀斯坛里。每个坛盖都是一位保护神的形状。尸体留在这里风干40天。然后会对其进行清洗、涂油和涂香料，再填入防腐剂。接着，尸体会用被松油浸透的亚麻布多层包裹，以保持其不变形。一个装饰性的面具会放在头部，最后整具尸体放入棺材。棺材都装饰得十分华丽。

procedure *n.* 程序；步骤

spice *n.* 香料

lid *n.* 盖子

An *elaborate* ceremony marked the burial of a pharaoh. The decorated coffin, plus the canopic jars, were carried to the pyramid. A procession of *mourners* was led by priests and priestesses. Following the mourners were servants who carried all the items meant to *accompany* the pharaoh into the next life—food, clothes, furniture, and more. Before burying the dead pharaoh, the body's mouth was opened by a priest. This practice was believed to allow the person to breathe, eat, and speak in the next life. Then the coffin was placed in the tomb and *sealed* inside the pyramid, in a chamber designed to keep it safe.

Do You Know?

Pharaohs were buried with statues of their servants. These statues, called shabtis, were believed to come to life in the next world so that the servant could once again serve the pharaoh.

人们用精心制作的仪式纪念法老的入葬。布置精美的棺材和克诺珀斯坛一起被搬到金字塔。送葬者们由几位男女祭司在前面引领着。在送葬者身后是仆人们，他们负责搬运法老来生所用的物品，包括食物、衣服、家具等等。在埋葬法老之前，尸体的嘴要由一位祭司打开。这种做法是因为人们相信这样可以使死者来生呼吸、吃饭和讲话。然后棺材就被放进坟墓，在金字塔内进行密封，放置到预先选好的墓室以保障其安全。

你知道吗？

法老仆人们的雕像要和法老一道埋葬。这些雕像叫作沙布俑，人们相信沙布俑在另一个世界会复活，这样就可以继续侍奉法老。

---

elaborate *adj.* 精心制作的
accompany *v.* 伴随或跟随（某人）

mourner *n.* 哀悼者
seal *v.* 密封；封住

Famous Egyptian Pyramids

The first pyramid, built for King Zoser at Saqqâra, is called a step pyramid because it had steps up the sides. Later pyramids had smaller steps. The design eventually changed into straight-sided pyramids, such as the Great Pyramid at Giza, which was built about 4,500 years ago for King Khufu. The Great Pyramid is 147 meters (482 ft.) tall and contains about 2,300,000 blocks of stone.

The Great Pyramid at Giza is part of a *complex* of pyramids built by King Khufu, his son Khafre, and grandson Menkaure. Their pyramids are surrounded by other pyramids for their queens, as well

著名的埃及金字塔

第一座金字塔是位于萨卡拉的昭赛尔金字塔，它被称作"阶梯金字塔"，因为它的四面都是阶梯状的。它之后的金字塔阶梯就小得多了。逐渐地设计最终发展成平面的金字塔，比如说吉萨的大金字塔，它是4500年前为胡夫国王建造的金字塔。这座大金字塔高147米（合482英尺），所用巨石达230万块。

吉萨大金字塔是为胡夫国王、其子哈佛拉国王和其孙门卡乌拉国王

complex *n.* 建筑群

as stone mastabas—tombs made of mud bricks—for the rest of the royal family and members of the court. The Sphinx, a limestone statue with the face of a king and the body of a lion, guards the entire site. The Sphinx represents the sun god.

All of the ancient Egyptian pyramids have had their treasures looted. Very few tombs have been left undisturbed. The only *intact* burial of an Egyptian king ever found is that of King Tutankhamen. His tomb, in the Valley of the Kings in Egypt, was built underground, rather than inside a pyramid. Because it was found intact, it has helped archaeologists to learn a great deal about the culture of ancient Egypt.

所建的系列金字塔建筑群中的一座。他们的金字塔被其皇后的金字塔所环绕，周围还有一些给其余皇室成员和宫廷成员建造的坟墓——这些坟墓是用泥砖建造的。狮身人面像是一座石灰石雕像，形为狮身，面为国王。它保卫着整个金字塔所在区域。狮身人面像代表的是太阳神。

所有古埃及金字塔的财富都曾遭掠夺。几乎没有哪座墓穴未被入侵过。目前发现唯一完好的古埃及国王墓穴是图坦卡门国王的。他的墓穴建在"帝王谷"的地下，而非建于金字塔内。因为这座墓穴发现时完好无损，它帮助考古学家了解到了大量关于古埃及的文化。

---

intact *adj.* 无损伤的；完整的

Pyramids in Other Lands

Pyramids were also built in the Americas. They were first built in Central America and in northwestern South America, but soon the practice of building pyramids *spread* to North America as well. Several of the New World cultures that built pyramids are mentioned below.

The Mayan people and other cultures in Central America built stepped pyramids. These pyramids had stairways decorated with sculptures and *inscriptions* that led to temples at the top. Sometimes, but not always, these pyramids contained the tombs of kings. One of the most famous Mayan pyramids is Chichén Itzá. Rebuilt over an

其他地方的金字塔

在美洲也建有金字塔。美洲的金字塔最早建立在中美洲或南美洲的西北部，但是金字塔的建造方法很快也传到了北美洲。以下就是几个新的世界文化中有建立金字塔的记录。

在中美洲的玛雅人和其他文化的人们建造了带阶梯的金字塔。这些金字塔用雕塑和铭文来装饰从塔底直到塔顶寺庙的阶梯。有时候但并不总是，这些金字塔内会有国王的墓室。最著名的玛雅金字塔之一就是奇琴

spread *v.* 传播；流传蔓延   inscription *n.* 题名；铭文

earlier pyramid, the current one was built just before A.D. 1100. The earlier one, built 100 years before,Chichén Itzá, the most famous Mayan pyramid. contained a stone sculpture of a jaguar that was painted red and had eyes made of jade. The jaguar, a Mayan symbol of the earth's fertility, was *worshipped* as a god.

The Aztecs, another Central American culture, built the Great Pyramid Temple, most likely in the 1300s, in their capital city of Tenochtitlán, on an island in Lake Texcoco in southcentral Mexico. The Aztecs believed that the sun god needed blood from human hearts to stay strong. Without human blood, the sun would die and the world would come to an end. Human *sacrifices* of prisoners taken

---

伊察。这座金字塔是在之前一座的基础上重建的，建造时间略早于公元1100年。而之前的一座，建造时间只为此前一百年，奇琴伊察，最著名的玛雅金字塔，内有一只美洲虎的石雕，眼为玉制，全身红色。美洲虎象征着玛雅的土地的肥沃，被玛雅人作为神来崇拜。

　　阿兹特克是另一种中美洲文化，他们建造了大金字塔神殿。时间大约是14世纪，地点在其首府特诺奇蒂特兰城，在墨西哥中南部的特斯科科湖的一个小岛上。阿兹特克人相信太阳神需要从人的心脏获得血液以保持强壮。如果没有人血，太阳就会死去，世界末日就会来临。在阿兹特克人的

---

worship *v.* 崇敬或热爱（上帝）　　　　　　　sacrifice *n.* 供品；祭品；牺牲

in war were a *regular* part of Aztec life, and these sacrifices took place at the Great Pyramid Temple.

Cultures in northwestern South America also built flat-topped, stepped pyramids. The Moche people, who *flourished* between 100 B.C. and A.D. 800, built the Pyramid of the Sun and the Pyramid of the Moon. About 600 to 700 years later, the Inca people built pyramids. The Temple of the Sun was the most sacred shrine in the Incan empire. It contained a huge gold disk that symbolized the sun god. The Incas believed that their rulers were direct *descendants* of the sun.

The pyramid shape has also been used in building designs in

生活中，用战犯来祭祀是很常见的，祭祀通常就在大金字塔神殿举行。

南美洲西北部的文化中也建造了平顶、带阶梯的金字塔。公元前100年到公元800年间是莫契人的鼎盛时期。他们建造了太阳金字塔和月亮金字塔。大约600至700年以后，印加人也建造了金字塔。太阳神殿是印加帝国最神圣的地方，内有一个巨大的金盘象征着太阳神。印加人相信他们的统治者就是太阳的后裔。

金字塔形也出现在世界其他文化的建筑设计中。在欧洲、亚洲和中东都可以找到金字塔形的设计。这种设计还用在了法国、英国、美国等国家

---

regular *adj.* 正常的；经常的　　　　　　flourish *v.* 昌盛；繁荣
descendant *n.* 后代；后裔

other cultures around the world. Pyramid designs can be found in parts of Europe, Asia, and the Middle East. The pyramid shape is also used in modern architecture in many countries, including France, England, and the United States. A modern pyramid was also built in Egypt to honor President Anwar Sadat, who was *assassinated* in 1981.

Conclusion

Efforts are being made to preserve and protect the pyramids of ancient Egypt, as well as pyramids in other parts of the world. Pollution, urban *expansion*, tourism, and other problems threaten the pyramids at Giza. The Great Pyramid of Khufu at Giza is the only one of the famous "Seven Wonders of the Ancient World" that still stands.

的现代建筑中。在埃及还有一座现代建造的金字塔，用以纪念其1981年遭到暗杀的总统安瓦尔·萨达特。

小结

现在已经有了措施用以保护古埃及金字塔以及世界其他地方的金字塔。环境污染、城市扩张、旅游业以及其他的问题都威胁到了吉萨的多座金字塔。在"古代文明七大奇迹"中，吉萨的胡夫大金字塔是唯一现存于世的了。

---

assassinate *v.* 暗杀；行刺　　　　　　expansion *n.* 扩大；扩展

All of the pyramids and tombs from ancient Egypt are wonders worthy of *preservation*. By studying pyramids, we learn about a complex and fascinating ancient culture and the accomplishments of humans who lived during that time. We also learn how an ancient culture honored its leaders and worshiped its gods.

古埃及所有的金字塔与墓穴都是值得保护的文明奇迹。通过研究金字塔，我们了解了复杂灿烂的古代文化以及生活在那个时代人类所取得的成就。我们也了解到古时文化是如何向他们的领袖致敬，向神灵表达崇拜的。

preservation *n.* 保护

M Is for Mexico

Welcome to Mexico! I am so glad you have come to visit my beautiful country. Mexico has a lot of rich history and culture. The people who live here are very kind, and their *hospitality* is out of this world!

M代表墨西哥

欢迎来到墨西哥！我很高兴你们能来游览我美丽的国家。墨西哥历史悠久，文化丰富。生活在这里的人民十分友善，他们的热情好客也是无可比拟的。

---

hospitality *n.* 殷勤好客；热情友好

There is so much here to see and do. The question is not what you want to do, but whether you will have the time to do it all. You might want to relax on the *shores* of Mexico's many beaches or visit some of our wonderful museums, historic sites, or ancient ruins. You could even go for a horseback ride in the mountains, a boat ride through the wetlands, or listen to local *mariachi* music. Whatever you want to do or see, Mexico has something for you!

The Land

Let's begin our tour by learning a little bit about Mexico's geography.

Mexico is located at the southern part of North America. The United States is its neighbor to the north. Guatemala and Belize are its neighbors to the south. The country is divided into North and

---

在这里，你可以游览很多地方，做很多事。问题不在于你想做些什么，而在于你是否有时间把想做的事情都做完。你或许想在众多墨西哥海滩的海岸上休息，参观那些令人惊叹的博物馆，历史遗址或远古遗迹。你还可以在山上骑马，在湿地里划船，抑或是聆听当地的墨西哥街头音乐。不管你想看些什么，做些什么，墨西哥总有你想要的！

土地

在旅行的开始，我们先了解一点墨西哥的地理知识。

墨西哥位于北美洲的南部。其北部与美国接壤，南接危地马拉和伯利兹。和美洲一样，墨西哥被分为南北两部分。在墨西哥南部，大多数州拥

---

shore *n.* 海岸；河岸；湖滨　　　　　　　mariachi *n.* 墨西哥流浪乐队

South, just like the Americas. In southern Mexico, most states have large *rural* areas with a large farming population. The northern states are wealthier than the southern states and are mostly *urban* and industrialized.

More than half of the country's population lives in the central part of the country. This area is what is called the Valley of Mexico. Mexico City, Mexico's capital, is in the valley. It is one of the ten largest cities in the world! About 18,131,000 people live in the Mexico City area while about 106 million people live in the entire country of Mexico.

The land in Mexico covers 756,066 square miles. How big is

有大片的农田，农业人口众多。墨西哥北部各州大多数是城市化和工业化地区，较南部来说更为富裕。

墨西哥半数以上人口居住在中部地区，此区被称为墨西哥谷地。墨西哥首都墨西哥城也位于该区域。墨西哥城是世界上最大的十座城市之一！墨西哥人口106 000 000，而墨西哥城居民就有约18 131 000人。

墨西哥国土面积达756 066平方英里。那是多大呢？这么说吧，墨西哥的面积是美国的1/5。我敢说你也不知道墨西哥是按州来划分区域的。

---

rural *adj.* 乡下的；乡村的   urban *adj.* 城市的；城镇的；都市的

that? Well, you could fit about five countries the size of Mexico into the United States. I *bet* you didn't know that Mexico has states, too. It has 31 states and a federal district. All of these areas have totally cool places to visit! Mexico's blue water and landforms are as diverse as its people and culture.

Mexico's many unique landform regions include the Mexican *plateau*, the central plateau, Gulf Coastal Plain, Pacific Coastal Lowlands, southern highlands, Chiapas Highlands, Tabasco Plain, the Yucatán *Peninsula*, Sierra Madre Occidental and Sierra Madre Oriental, and the Sonoran Desert. If you review that list, you'll notice that very few sound alike.

该国有31个州和1个联邦地区。这些地区都有值得游览的好地方。墨西哥蔚蓝的海水和地形地貌与它的人口和文化一样，极具多元化。

墨西哥许多地区地貌独特，它们包括墨西哥高原、中部高原、墨西哥湾沿岸平原、太平洋沿岸低地、南部高地、奇阿帕斯高地（Chiapas Highland）、塔巴斯克平原（Tabasco plain）、尤卡坦半岛(the Yucatán Peninsula)、西马德雷山脉（Sierra Madre Occidental）、东马德雷山脉（Sierra Madre Oriental）和索诺拉沙漠（the Sonoran Desert）。如果回顾一下这个清单，你会发现这些地名各具特色。

---

bet *v.* 打赌；下注
peninsula *n.* 半岛

plateau *n.* 高原

Do You Know?

Volcán Pico de Orizaba has not *erupted* since 1687. No one climbed it until 1848. The volcano is the third highest in North America. Do you know what the first two highest points are?

Since Mexico is a diverse land, it ranks third in the world for the most varied plant and animal *species*. Did you know that Mexico is also in the "Ring of Fire"? That means that it is located in an area where volcanoes in the Pacific Ocean are very active. I hope you will take the time to visit Mexico's Volcán Pico de Orizaba. This is a fascinating *dormant* volcano and the country's highest point. It rises to 18,406 feet (5,610 meters).

From cities to rural areas, from deserts to rainforests, from wetlands to canyons, Mexico has every kind of environment you're looking for! Let's explore more about my country.

你知道吗?

奥里萨巴山（Volcán Pico de Orizaba）自1687年后就再也没有喷发过。1848年以前没有人登过此山。这座火山是北美第三大高峰，你知道其他两座更高的山峰是哪里吗？

由于其多元化的地形，墨西哥在世界动植物种类多样性地区中排名第三。你知道墨西哥也位于"环太平洋火山地区"吗？这代表它位于太平洋火山活动强烈的地区。我想你应趁此机会游览奥里萨巴山。这是一座迷人的休眠火山，也是国家的最高峰，其高度达18 406英尺（5 610米）。

从城市到乡村，沙漠到雨林，湿地到峡谷，墨西哥一定有你在寻找的每种环境！一起近一步探索我的国家吧。

---

erupt *v.* （火山）喷发；爆发

dormant *adj.* 暂停活动的；休眠的

species *n.* 物种；种

When to Visit

One thing to keep in mind is that Mexico's *climate* along the coast is hot and *humid*. If you don't like hot and humid weather, you should plan your trip from October through May. Of course, the *temperatures* are almost always *milder* inland and in the mountains. If you love dry weather, try visiting Baja California or the Sonoran or Chihuahuan deserts. It is dry in these places year-round.

My Country's History

Before the Spanish defeated the Aztecs in 1521, Mexico was part of what is called Mesoamerica. The Olmecs, Maya, Teotihuacán, Toltec, and the Aztec peoples lived in Mesoamerica for a long time before the Spanish arrived. This period of history is called the pre-Columbian period. You can visit some of the buildings they left

---

何时去参观

有一件事情得记住——墨西哥沿岸气候炎热潮湿。如果不喜欢这样的天气，你可以把旅行计划放到10月份到次年5月份。当然了，墨西哥内陆和山地气候总是较为温和。如果你喜欢干燥的天气，可以去巴扎加利福尼亚（Baja California），索诺拉沙漠（Sonoran）或奇瓦瓦沙漠（Chihuahuan deserts）游玩。这些地区气候常年干燥。

祖国的历史

西班牙人于1521年打败阿兹特克人（the Aztecs），在那之前，墨西哥是中美洲的一部分。在西班牙人到来之前，奥尔梅克人（the

---

climate *n.* 气候
temperature *n.* 温度；气温

humid *adj.* （空气、气候）潮湿的；湿热的
mild *adj.* 温和的；不强烈的；不严重的

behind such as temples, pyramids, and even ball courts!

The Aztecs were the most powerful of the pre-Columbian *civilizations*. After the Spanish arrived and *conquered* the Aztecs, not only did the people change, but also our land. Spain sent some of its people to live here. The Spaniards made the *indigenous* people become Catholics. They had to learn Spanish and Latin, and many of the native languages disappeared. Today Spanish is the *official* language of Mexico. Mexico was a colony of Spain until 1810. Many Mexicans revolted against Spain, and in 1821, Mexico officially won its independence. It is now a republic.

Olmecs）、玛雅人（the Maya）、特奥蒂瓦坎人（the Teotihuacn）、托尔特克人（the Toltec）和阿兹特克人在中美洲居住了相当长一段时间。这段历史时期叫作前哥伦布时期。你可以参观那时留下的建筑，例如：神殿、金字塔，甚至球场！

在前哥伦布文明中，阿兹特克人最为强大。在西班牙人到达并征服阿兹特克后，不仅教化了当地的居民，也令这一片土地发生了变化。西班牙人让自己的部分居民居住在此，并令当地土著居民信奉天主教。土著居民们不得不学习西班牙语和拉丁语，许多当地语言因此绝迹了。现在，西班牙语为墨西哥官方语言。一直到1810年以前，墨西哥一直是西班牙的殖

---

civilization *n.* 文明社会
indigenous *adj.* 当地的；本土的

conquer *v.* 占领；征服
official *adj.* 官方的；正式的

Explore More

In addition to the Aztecs, the Olmecs, Maya, Teotihuacán, and Toltecs also lived in Mesoamerica. Find out more about these cultures and civilizations by searching the Internet or your local library.

Mexico City

Now, let's begin our tour of some of the great cities to visit. We'll begin in the heart of Mexico— Mexico City. When the Aztecs ruled, it was called Tenochtitlán. Many of the ancient ruins in and around

民地。许多墨西哥人奋起反抗西班牙统治，墨西哥终于在1821年正式独立，成为共和国。

探索更多

除了阿兹特克人以外，奥尔梅克人、玛雅人、特奥蒂瓦坎人和托尔特克人都曾在中美洲地区居住过。你可以在网络上或当地图书馆中，查找更多有关这些文化和文明的信息。

墨西哥城

现在，让我们先来游览一些大城市。我们将首先来到墨西哥的心脏地

in addition to 除……之外

Mexico City were built by the Aztecs. The Templo Mayor (Great Temple) was actually the site of the capital of the Aztec Empire. It was built during the 1300s and 1400s. The Spanish tried to *bury* it, but in 1978 the amazing temple's ruins were uncovered. It is now a museum.

In Mexico City, there are also many beautiful things to see that were built under Spanish rule. Cathedrals and other examples of Spanish *architecture* are all over Mexico City. The largest cathedral in Latin America is Cathedral Metropolitana. Would you believe it took nearly 300 years to build?

Throughout the city you can see painted or *sculpted* art by famous Mexican artists. One of the most well-known is muralist Diego

区——墨西哥城。在阿兹特克人统治时期，它叫作特诺奇提特兰。墨西哥城内和附近的许多古遗址都是当时的阿兹特克人所建造的。玛雅神庙（大神庙）原来是阿兹特克帝国首都的地址，修建于14至15世纪之间。后来西班牙人曾试图将它掩埋。但在1978年，这座令人叹为观止的神庙遗址被人们发现。现在，它成了一座博物馆。

在墨西哥城，你也可以欣赏到许多西班牙统治时期的美丽建筑。大教堂和其他西班牙风格的建筑遍布墨西哥城。拉丁美洲最大的教堂要属主座教堂（Cathedral Metropolitana）。你能想象人们花了近三百年来建造这座教堂吗？

在整座城市里，你都可以看到墨西哥著名艺术家的画作和雕塑作品。

bury *v.* 掩埋；埋藏　　　　　　architecture *n.* 建筑式样；建筑风格
sculpt *v.* 做塑像或雕像

Rivera. From 1929 to 1935, he painted *murals* showing Mexican history in the courtyard of the Palacio Nacional, or National Palace.

The site of the palace has been home to many rulers. Moctezuma, who was an Aztec *emperor*, lived on the same site before the Spanish conquest. After the Spanish conquest, it was home to Spanish conquistador Hernán Cortés. Today, the offi ces of Mexico's president are inside. The palace faces the Plaza de la Constitución (Zócalo). This is one of the world's largest public squares.

Mexico City's largest park is another major attraction. This was where the Aztecs used to spend their summer vacations! You can spend a part of your vacation at Bosque de Chapultepec, too. You

迭戈·里维拉（Diego Rivera）就是最著名的壁画家之一。从1929年至1935年，他在墨西哥国家宫（Palacio Nacional）庭院里创作壁画，展示墨西哥的历史。

墨西哥国家宫曾被许多统治者作为宫殿。原阿兹特克的皇帝蒙特苏马（Moctezuma）在西班牙入侵前居住于此。在西班牙人来到之后，西班牙统治者荷南·科尔蒂斯（Hernán Cortés）也曾在此居住过。今天，墨西哥总统府位于此处。国家宫对面是宪法广场（Plaza de la Constitución），称为索卡洛（Zócalo，意为柱基）。它是世界上最大的公共广场之一。

墨西哥城最大的公园是另一处旅游胜地。这里曾是阿兹特克人度暑假的地方！你也可以在暑假期间到查普尔特佩克公园（Bosque de

mural *n.* 壁画　　　　　　　　　　　　　　　emperor *n.* 皇帝

can visit a zoo or *botanical* garden, buy a balloon or a *snack*, and then visit museums or art galleries and not even leave the park!

There are other art museums and centers throughout the city, including the Palacio de Bellas Artes, Museo Dolores Olmedo Patiño, Museo Mural Diego Rivera, Museo Frida Kahlo, and many, many more. Frida Kahlo was one of the first successful female painters in the world. She was married to Diego Rivera. My favorite painting of hers has a monkey in it!

However, if shopping is what you want to do while in Mexico City, you won't be disappointed at the Bazar del Sábado (Saturday

Chapultepec）游玩。你可以游览动植物园，买气球或小吃，然后去博物馆抑或是艺术馆，而且所有这些事你却可以不用离开公园就做到！

城内也有许多其他的美术博物馆和艺术中心，其中有墨西哥国家美术宫（Palacio de bellas artes）、Dolores Olmedo Patio博物馆、迭戈·里维拉壁画博物馆（Museo Mural Diego Rivera），以及弗里达·卡罗博物馆（Museo Frida Kahlo），还有许许多多其他的地方。弗里达·卡罗是世界上最成功的女画家之一。她的丈夫是迭戈·里维拉。她有一幅自画像中还画了一只小猴子，那是我最喜欢的弗里达的作品！

然后，如果你是想在墨西哥城购物，圣天使（San Ángel）街区的圣

botanical *adj.* 植物（学）的　　　　　　　　snack *n.* 快餐；小吃

Market) in the Plaza San Jacinto in the San Ángel neighborhood. You can buy Mexican fruits, vegetables, or even candy, at the Mercado de la Merced.

Central and Southern Mexico

Just northwest of Mexico City, you can find more great examples of Spanish colonial architecture. Sometimes this area is called the Colonial Heartland. It is also the heart of Mexico's rich agriculture. The Spanish built many cities and towns here because of the silver *deposits*. If you visit the city of Taxco, southwest of Mexico City, you can find many beautiful silver shops.

哈辛托广场（Plaza San Jacinto）的巴扎尔德尔市场（Bazar del Sábado）一定不会让你失望，它是一个周六营业的跳蚤市场。你也可以在梅尔塞市场（Mercado de la Merced）买些墨西哥水果、蔬菜，甚至是糖果。

墨西哥中部及南部

就在墨西哥城的西北处，你会看到更多的西班牙殖民建筑佳作。人们有时把这片区域称作"殖民中心区"，这里也是墨西哥富饶农业的心脏地带。由于此处蕴藏着银矿，墨西哥人曾在此建造了许多城镇。如果你去墨西哥西南部的城市——达斯科（Taxco），会看到许多精美的银饰店。

---

deposit *n.* 沉积物；矿床

Farther west there are many beaches. One place known for its beaches is Acapulco. Decades ago, Puerto Vallarta became a popular beach *resort* for Hollywood stars.

If you get tired of the beach, you can visit a pre-Columbian site in Colima. Colima has been rebuilt over and over again because *frequent* earthquakes continually *damage* it.

Guadalajara is the country's second largest city after Mexico City. There are many great places to visit in Guadalajara. There is the city's famous Cathedral, which took more than two centuries to

---

继续向西走，你会看到很多海滩。亚加布尔科（Acapulco）就是一个以海滩而闻名的城市。就在几十年前，巴亚尔塔港（Puerto Vallarta）就是好莱坞明星常去的海滩度假胜地。

如果看腻了海滩，那么就去科利马（Colima)参观前哥伦布时代的遗址。由于频繁而持续的遭受地震破坏，科利马经历过多次重建。

瓜达拉哈拉（Guadalajara）是墨西哥第二大城市，仅次于墨西哥城。在这里有很多地方可以观光。这里有历时两个多世纪建造的一座著名的大

---

resort *n.* 度假；胜地　　　　　　　　　　frequent *adj.* 经常性的；频繁的
damage *v.* 损坏；破坏；毁坏

build. You can take a short walk from the Cathedral and see a lot of Spanish colonial architecture.

But like many regions in Mexico, you can also just enjoy being outside! The country's largest lake, Laguna de Chapala, is a great place to go boating. You may want to check out the waterfalls, *tropics*, and mountains at Huasteca Potosina. I *recommend* that you take a boat ride to see Tamul waterfall. It drops 344 feet into a canyon!

教堂。从大教堂再走一小段路，你还可以看见很多西班牙殖民时期的建筑。

但就像墨西哥许多地方一样，在户外也同样乐趣无穷！墨西哥最大的湖——查帕拉湖（Laguna de Chapala），是划船的好去处。如果你想看看华斯特克——波多斯那区域(Huasteca Potosina)的瀑布、热带地区和山脉，我推荐你乘船去看泰木尔瀑布(Tamul)。瀑布高度达344英尺，一直俯冲至下面的峡谷中。

---

tropics *n.* 热带（地区）   recommend *v.* 推荐；介绍

Central and southern Mexico have many ancient ruins of pre-Columbian civilizations. Teotihuacán (tay-uh-tee-wah- KAHN) is probably one of the greatest examples of all pre-Columbian cities. It has two great ancient temples: the Pyramids of the Sun and the Moon, which people visit more than any other pre-Columbian site.

So what was Teotihuacán? It was once a place where about 125,000 people lived in about A.D. 400. And it is also the name of the people who lived there. Kind of *confusing* , huh? At that time, it was one of the world's largest cities.

Monte Albán in the state of Oaxaca was a city of the Zapotec people. You can visit what was their ceremonial site on top of a

---

墨西哥中部和南部有许多前哥伦布时期的古遗址。特奥蒂瓦坎 (Teotihuacán) 在所有前哥伦布时期的城市中，或许是一座最有代表性的城市。来这里有两座古代神庙：太阳金字塔和月亮金字塔。来这里的游客远比去其他前哥伦布遗址的游客多。

那么特奥蒂瓦坎是怎样一座城市呢？公元400年左右，约12 5000人居住于此。这里的居民也叫特奥蒂瓦坎。不太好分辨，是吧？当时，它可是世界上最大的城市之一。

瓦哈卡州 (Oaxaca) 的阿尔班山 (Monte Albán)为萨巴特克人 (Zapotec)居住区 。你可以去山顶上看看，那是他们以前举行仪式的地

---

confusing *adj.* 令人困惑的；混乱的

mountain! At one time, this was also a cultural center for the Olmec and the Teotihuacán.

Moving out to the tropical plains and *jungle* of the Gulf Coast, we find land that was once home to several pre-Columbian cultures, including the Maya, Olmec, and Totonac. Olmec *artifacts* are all over this region, especially in the Parque-Museo de La Venta.

You can visit ancient pyramids at El Tajin. This was a major religious center for the Totonac who lived here between A.D. 900 and 1150. Or you can *check out* Quiahuiztlán, a hilltop city where some 15,000 Totonac people once lived.

方！这里曾经是奥尔梅克人(Olmec)和特奥蒂瓦坎人的文化中心。

继续前往墨西哥湾的热带平原和丛林，我们就来到了这样一片土地，它孕育了包括玛雅、奥尔梅克、托托纳克（Totonac)在内的数个前哥伦布时期的文化。这里到处都能看见奥尔梅克手工制品，特别是在拉文塔博物馆（La Venta）里，你能看到更多。

你可以去埃尔塔津古城观赏古代金字塔。公元900年到1150年，托托纳克人居住于此，这里是他们主要的宗教中心。你也可以去基亚乌依兹特兰(Quiahuiztlán)，这是一座位于山顶的城市，大概15000名托托纳克人曾居住于此。

jungle *n.* 热带森林；密林   artifact *n.* 人工制品，手工艺品
check out （口）看看

The Mayan ruins at Chichen Itza are the best *preserved* of anything the Maya left behind. There are temples, Mexico's largest ancient ball court, and an *observatory*. The Maya were *fascinated* with looking at the stars, just like me! They even had their own writing system. Uxmal is another Mayan site that you should visit. Most of the Spanish cities and towns in the Yucatán were actually built on top of Mayan ruins.

What other cool things are there to see and do on the Gulf Coast? Just about everything! There are many museums, cathedrals, and churches. Don't forget to stop in the city of El Puerto Veracruz! The waterfront *promenade* and arcades are a lot of fun.

奇琴伊察（Chichen Itza）是玛雅现存遗址中保存最完好的。这里有神庙，墨西哥最大的古代球场，还有一个观象台。玛雅人痴迷于观察天象，我也是！他们甚至有自己的书写系统。另一处不可错过的玛雅遗址是乌斯马尔（Uxmal）。实际上，尤卡坦地区大多数的西班牙城镇都是建造在玛雅遗址上面的。

墨西哥湾地区还有什么有趣的事等着你去看去做呢？答案是所有的！这里有许多博物馆、大教堂和小教堂。别忘了在维拉克鲁斯（El Puerto

---

preserved *adj.* 可保存的   observatory *n.* 天文台；观象台
fascinate *v.* （使）着迷；陶醉   promenade *n.* 滨海大道

Like the Colonial Heartland, this region is also a center for agriculture. Sugarcane, cocoa (yum!), and coffee are grown here.

The Yucatán Peninsula is also well known for its white sand beaches, and has plenty of them considering it's surrounded by water on three sides, like Baja California. The world's second longest barrier reef (after Australia's) is located near the islands of Cozumel and Isla Mujeres. It is a popular place to snorkel and *scuba dive*. Cancún is probably the most popular spot to get a *suntan*. This region is well-known for its breathtaking natural wells called cenotes. Probably the most visited one is the Cenote de Dzitnup near Valladolid. Can you believe that it was discovered only a half century

---

Veracruz）小歇一下！这里的海边长廊和商场乐趣无穷。

这片区域，和殖民中心区一样，也是农业中心。这里种植着甘蔗、可可豆（好吃！）和咖啡豆。

尤卡坦半岛三面环海（如巴扎加利福尼亚），有大片的白色沙滩——这里的白沙滩非常有名。可祖梅尔岛（Cozumel）和女人岛（Isla Mujeres）附近有世界第二长的大堡礁（仅次于澳大利亚）。这里是潜泳和潜水的胜地。要是想把肌肤晒得黝黑，坎昆（Cancún）大概是不二选择了。该地区有着壮观的天然井，举世闻名。人们最常游览的地方是巴利亚多利德（Valladolid）附近的兹特那普地下湖(Cenote de Dzitnup)。你能相

---

scuba dive 水肺潜水   suntan *n.* 晒黑

ago?

Northern Mexico

Many of Mexico's deserts, mountains, and canyons are located here. You might have heard of the Grand Canyon in the United States, but did you know that Copper Canyon is even bigger? It is more than one mile deep and part of the Sierra Madre Occidental range. You can take a train to get a close-up view of this deep canyon, its waterfalls, and lakes. The indigenous people who live there *are famous for* the drums and violins they make.

If you are looking for great beaches and resorts, like Cabo San Lucas, then Baja California is the place for you. It is a peninsula, so

---

信它是半个世纪前才被发现的吗？

墨西哥北部

墨西哥许多沙漠、山脉和大峡谷都位于此地。你可能听说过美国的科罗拉多大峡谷，但你知道吗？大铜谷比它还要大。大铜谷深度超过了一英里，是西马德雷山脉的一部分。你可以坐火车近距离观赏这个大峡谷，看看众多的瀑布和湖泊。当地土著居民以其制造的鼓和小提琴而闻名于世。

如果你在找像卡伯圣卢卡斯（Cabo San Lucas）一样的海滩和度假胜地，那么巴扎加利福尼亚绝对是个好去处。这个半岛三面环海。在冬季鲸

---

be famous for 以……而著名

water is around three of its sides. In the winter, you can even *spot* whales swimming along the shore as they migrate south!

You won't find any Aztec ruins in Baja. Why? Because the Aztecs did not live here! But you can find some ancient cave paintings. Many believe the ancestors of the Cochimi painted the cave pictures. They show people and animals in black and red.

Probably the most amazing ancient ruins in this region are the adobe buildings at Paquimé. Adobe is a brick made with mud and grass. Often many bricks were used to create buildings that look like today's *apartment* buildings. Between the 900s and 1300s, more than 3,000 people lived in adobe buildings near the Casas Grandes river.

鱼南迁时，你还能看到它们在你眼前游过海岸！

在巴扎，你找不到任阿兹特克遗迹。为什么呢？因为阿兹特克人没有在此居住过！但是在这你能发现一些洞穴壁画。许多人认为，科奇米人（Cochimi）的祖先创作了这些洞穴壁画。他们用红黑两色就塑造了人类及动物的形象。

也许，该地区最令人惊叹的古代遗迹是大卡萨斯（Paquimé）的土坯建筑。土坯是一种由泥土和草制成的砖块。大量的砖块盖起的楼群和现在的公寓楼看起来差不多。在10世纪到14世纪之间，3 000多居民住在大卡

---

spot *v.* 发现　　　　　　　　　　　apartment *n.* 寓所；住房；公寓

No one really knows what happened to the people who lived there.

If you're not interested in ruins or the beach, you may enjoy whale watching in a boat. In Guerrero Negro, blue whales are often spotted along the Sea of Cortés. If you get *seasick*, you can visit them and many other sea mammals on land at the nearby Laguna San Ignacio, Bahia de Magdalena.

There are also many old Spanish missions in this region. One you can visit is called San Ignacio. It is a *mission* church from the 1700s. The Museo de las Misiones is part of Misión Nuestra Señora

---

萨斯河（Casas Granges)附近的土坯建筑中。没有人知道住在那里的居民发生了什么事情。

如果你对遗址和沙滩不感兴趣，你可以乘船观赏鲸鱼。在黑格雷罗（Guerrero Negro)，人们总能在科尔蒂斯海（Sea of Cortés）地区看到蓝鲸。如果你晕船，也可以就在马格达勒那海湾(Bahia de Magdalena)附近的圣伊格纳西奥湖（Laguna San Ignacio）观赏到鲸鱼和其他在陆地上活动的海洋哺乳动物们。

该地区也有许多旧时西班牙的教会。你可以去圣伊格纳西奥（San

---

seasick *adj.* 晕船的   mission *n.* 布道所；传教区

de Loreto. The Spanish built the missions in an effort to convert the indigenous people to Catholicism.

I think you have to *agree with me*: Mexico has much to offer you— so come visit!

Quick Facts About Mexico

People

Ethnic groups: mestizo/Amerindian (90%), white (9%), other (1%)

Ignacio），这个宣道教会始建于18世纪。米西奥斯内斯博物馆(The Museo de las Misiones)就是洛雷托圣母教会(Misión Nuestra Señora de Loreto)的一部分。西班牙人为了让当地人信奉天主教，就修建了这些教会。

我想你也会同意我的看法：墨西哥有太多令你着迷的地方——那么快来看看吧！

墨西哥快览

人口

民族：印欧混血/美洲印第安人（90%），白种人（9%），其他（1%）

---

agree with sb 同意某人的看法

Religion:	Roman *Catholic* (89%), Protestant (6%), other (5%)
Languages:	Spanish, Mayan, Nahuatl, other

Government

Chief of State:	President Vincente Fox (since 2000)
Congress:	Senate: 128 seats;
	Chamber of Deputies: 500 seats

Economics

Currency:	peso
Natural resources:	*petroleum*, silver, copper, gold, lead, zinc, natural gas, timber

---

宗教：罗马天主教(89%)，新教（6%），其他（5%）
语言：西班牙语、玛雅语、纳瓦特尔语，及其他
政体
国家元首：比森克·福克斯总统（2000年至今）
国会：参议院128席位
　　　众议院500席位
经济
货币：比索
自然资源：石油、银、铜、金、铅、锌、天然气、木材

Catholic *n.* 天主教　　　　　　　　　　　　petroleum *n.* 石油

Workforce:	agriculture (4%), industry (27.2%), services (68.9%)
Farm products:	corn, wheat, soybeans, rice, beans, cotton, coffee, fruit, tomatoes; beef, *poultry*, dairy products; wood products
Industries:	food and beverages, tobacco, chemicals, iron and steel, oil, mining, tourism
Exports:	manufactured goods, oil, silver, fruits and vegetables, coffee, cotton

[Source: 2005 CIA *World Fact Book*, *Encyclopaedia Britannica*]

劳动力组成：农业（4%），工业（27.2%），服务业（68.9%）

农产品：玉米、小麦、大豆、稻米、豆类、棉花、咖啡、水果、番茄、牛肉、家禽、奶制品、木制品

工业：餐饮业、烟草业、化工业、钢铁产业、石油工业、采矿业、旅游业

出口产品：加工产品、石油、银、蔬菜水果、咖啡、棉花

（资料来源：2005年美国中情局《世界概况》和《大英百科全书》）

---

poultry *n.* 家禽

The Roman Empire Faces Attila

Terror from Asia

No invaders in ancient Europe struck as much terror into people's hearts as the Huns. These *ferocious* horsemen from northcentral Asia thundered into the heart of Europe in the AD 370s. Wherever they went, they left death and destruction behind them. Historians of the time described the Huns as *hideous barbarians* who killed without mercy.

罗马帝国与阿提拉之间的较量

来自亚洲的恐惧

在古欧洲，没有其他入侵者能像匈奴人一样令人恐惧了。公元370年，这群来自中北亚的凶猛骑士们使欧洲人胆战心惊。他们所到之处，将死亡与毁坏抛在身后。当时的历史学家们称匈奴人为"可憎的杀人不眨眼的野蛮人"。

---

ferocious *adj.* 凶猛的；凶暴的 hideous *adj.* 令人惊骇的；可怕的
barbarian *n.* 野蛮人；未开化的人

The leader of the Huns when they were at the height of their reign of terror was a man named Attila (AT-uh-luh or uh-TIL-uh). The people of Europe found Attila so *horrifying* that they called him "the Scourge of God". Attila crushed nearly every army sent against him.

United We Stand

Beginning around 27 BC in Europe, the Roman armies *fanned out* and conquered much of the ancient world. The Roman Empire ruled as a united entity for close to five centuries. By the mid-300s, the empire was growing old and tired. The empire covered so much land that it took two emperors to govern it. One emperor ruled in the west from the city of Rome; the other—Valens— ruled in the east from Constantinople, a city in what is now the country of Turkey. By

---

在匈奴人的恐怖统治最为猖獗之时，其领袖是阿提拉。欧洲人极其畏惧阿提拉，他们称他为"上帝之鞭"。阿提拉几乎摧毁了所有与他为敌的队伍。

团结共存

大约在公元前27年，罗马军队在欧洲大陆呈扇形铺开，征服了古代世界的大部分地区。罗马帝国是一个统一的国家，存在了将近5个世纪。到4世纪中期，罗马帝国走向了衰落。罗马帝国的疆域非常广阔，以至于需要两个帝王来统治。一个帝王统治罗马城以西的地区；另一个帝王——瓦伦士——统治君士坦丁堡以东的地区。君士坦丁堡位于今天的土耳其。

---

horrifying *adj.* 令人恐惧的，使人惊骇的   fan out （呈扇形）展开；分开

the year 400, the two halves of the empire would be permanently divided and would never enjoy the power they had once enjoyed as one united empire.

In AD 376, a messenger brought some very disturbing news to Roman Emperor Valens. The messenger said that large numbers of Germanic people called the Visigoths were *swarming* into the Roman Empire. They were seeking protection from a terrible new enemy from the east: the Huns. This was the first time that the Roman world had heard *rumor* of the Huns.

The Visigoth *refugees* were allowed to settle in the Eastern Roman Empire. But the Romans treated them badly. The angry Visigoths rebelled. For two years, they *rampaged* through part of

---

到公元400年，帝国的两个部分永久地分裂了，再也无法拥有像从前统一时那样强大的实力了。

公元376年，信使为罗马帝国国王瓦伦士带来了令他心惊的消息。信使说大批叫作西哥特人的日耳曼族人涌入罗马帝国。他们是为躲避东方世界的可怕敌人——匈奴，前来寻求庇护。这是罗马人第一次听说有关匈奴人的传闻。

东罗马帝国允许西哥特王国的难民们在此定居，但是经常欺压这些难民。愤怒的西哥特人奋起反抗。两年来，他们在东罗马帝国部分地区引起暴乱，造成了大规模破坏。而暴乱和毁灭恰恰是他们当初想要避开的东

---

swarm *v.* （人）成群涌动；拥挤
refugee *n.* 难民；寻求庇护者

rumor *n.* （美）传闻
rampage *v.* 横冲直撞

the Eastern Empire, causing great destruction similar to what they were *fleeing*. Valens led an army to stop the uprising, but the Visigoths destroyed his army and Valens was killed.

Without the leadership of Valens, the Roman Empire became weaker. The Visigoths and other Germanic tribes began attacking the western part of the empire. Without a central leader, the Romans were powerless to stop the invaders. Nearly 40 years after the Visigoths first started fleeing the Huns, the Visigoths *sacked* the city of Rome in AD 410. Enemies had not destroyed the capital city in centuries. It was a *devastating* blow. The last thing the Romans needed at this point was even more trouble. But they were soon to get it, and it came from the Huns.

西。瓦伦士率领一支军队前来镇压这场暴乱。但是，西哥特人打垮了他的军队，并杀死了瓦伦士。

失去瓦伦士领导的罗马帝国逐渐衰败。西哥特王国和其他日耳曼部落开始进攻罗王帝国的西部地区。由于缺乏核心领导人，罗马人无力阻止这些入侵者。公元410年，西哥特人洗劫了罗马城。而这一年距他们最早逃离匈奴人不到40年。数百年来，罗马都城都未曾被攻破过，这次对他们是一个毁灭性的打击。此时的罗马人已经禁不起任何麻烦了。可是麻烦很快找上门——匈奴人把野心投向了古罗马。

---

flee *v.* 逃离；逃避
devastating *adj.* 毁灭性的；极具破坏力的

sack *v.* 掠夺

Nearly 100 years after the Visigoths sacked Rome, they and other Germanic tribes had taken over the land once governed by the Western Roman Empire.

The Scourge of God

The Huns had settled into an area that is now part of the country of Hungary. They built towns. The leaders lived in houses made of wood, but most of the people lived in tents. The tents *enabled* them to easily leave the settlement on horseback, taking their home with them. The Huns were not *content* with what they had. They wanted more.

The Huns wanted money and nice things, so they attacked people who had those things. Beginning in the 420s, they *demanded*

在西哥特人洗劫罗马城一百年之后，他们和其他日耳曼部落占领了原来西罗马帝国的领地。

上帝之鞭

匈奴人曾经定居的地区现在是匈牙利的领土。他们在那儿修建城镇。其首领住在木屋里，其他人住在帐篷里。帐篷很容易放在马背上，所以他们可以随时迁移。匈奴人不满足于现有的东西,他们想要的远远不止这些。

匈奴人想要金钱和值钱的东西，因此他们去进攻拥有这些东西的人。从5世纪20年代开始，匈奴人要求罗马人每年进贡几百磅的黄金。东罗马

---

enable *v.* 使能够；使有机会
demand *v.* （强烈）要求；强令

content *adj.* 满足的；满意的

an annual payment of several hundred pounds of gold each year from the Romans. *Desiring* to keep the peace, the new Eastern Roman emperor, Theodosius II (thee-uh- DOH-shee-us) agreed to the demand. For more than 20 years, the Huns accepted the payments and caused the Romans little trouble. That began to change in the AD 440s, after a man named Attila rose to become the *sole* ruler of the Huns and the Germanic people the Huns had conquered.

Attila was in his late 30s. A Germanic historian of the time described the new king: "He has small, deep-set eyes, a flat nose, a few hairs in the place of a beard, broad shoulders, and a short, square body." Other people who met Attila said he had very simple

---

帝国新国王狄奥多西二世为了维持和平，同意了他们的要求。20多年来，匈奴人收取贡金，很少找罗马人的麻烦。但从5世纪40年代起和平之势将告终结，因为一个叫阿提拉的人成了匈奴以及被匈奴人征服的日耳曼民族的唯一领袖。

此时，阿提拉还不到40岁。当时的一位日耳曼历史学家是这样描述这位新帝王的："他眼睛小、眼窝深、鼻子扁平、胡须稀疏、肩膀宽、身材矮小健壮。"其他见过阿提拉的人说他爱好单一，饮食很有节制，参加盛宴的次数屈指可数。

---

desire *v.* 渴望；热望　　　　　　　　　sole *adj.* 孤独的；唯一的

tastes and ate and participated in *feasts* in *moderation*.

Attila might have been moderate when relaxing with friends, but he was ferocious when dealing with the Romans. He demanded more gold from them. In order to maintain peace, Theodosius agreed to double the annual payment, but then Attila wanted even more. With an army of about 100,000 men, Attila *launched* war against the eastern part of the Roman Empire. The Huns reduced one Roman city after another to ruins and killed many thousands of people.

To stop the destruction and killing, Theodosius agreed to once again double the annual payment of gold. The Huns would now get about 950 kilograms (2,100 pounds) of gold each year. But when Theodosius died in AD 450, the new Eastern Roman emperor,

---

阿提拉可能跟朋友在一起放松时很温和，但他对付起罗马人就会特别残忍。他命令罗马人进贡更多的黄金。狄奥多西为了维持和平，同意加倍进贡，但阿提拉欲壑难填，最终率领十万人的部队向东罗马帝国开战。匈奴人摧毁了一座又一座罗马城，杀害了成千上万人。

狄奥多西为了阻止毁灭和杀戮，再次同意加倍进贡黄金。匈奴人现在每年能够得到大约950公斤（2 100磅）的黄金。但公元450年狄奥多西去世时，东罗马帝国新国王马尔西安决定不再向匈奴人进贡。这使得阿提拉

---

feast n. 宴会；筵席
launch v. 发起；发动（军事袭击等）

moderation n. 适度；自我节制

Marcian (MAR-shun), refused to make any further payments. That put Attila into a rage, and he took his *fury* out on the Western Roman Empire.

Walls like these were built around the Eastern Roman Empire's capital, Constantinople, to keep invaders like Attila from taking over the city.

A Lady in Distress

Historians theorize that Attila may have had several reasons for turning his attention to the western part of the empire. He may have decided that Marcian was someone he didn't want to anger. Attila had also already *drained* the eastern part of the empire of much of its wealth. Both of these reasons made the Western Roman Empire an *inviting* target.

大发雷霆，但他把怒火烧到了西罗马帝国。

东罗马帝国在国都君士坦丁堡周围修建城墙阻止像阿提拉这样的入侵者攻占城市。

绝望的女人

历史学家们推论,阿提拉把注意力转向西罗马帝国有几个原因。可能是他不愿去招惹马尔西安，再说阿提拉已经几乎把东罗马帝国的财富给榨干了。这两条原因都使西罗马帝国成为了一个诱人的目标。

---

fury *n.* 狂怒；暴怒　　　　　　drain *v.* 使（精力、金钱）耗尽
inviting *adj.* 诱人的

Attila had never needed an excuse for attacking. He just did it and took what he wanted. But this time, he pretended that he had an excuse. Honoria (ho-NOR-ee-uh), sister of the Western emperor, Valentinian III, had written to him. Honoria had been discovered having a secret *romance* with a servant. The servant was *executed*, and Honoria was locked away. Desperate to be free, she sent a letter to Attila begging him for help. She enclosed her ring as proof that she wrote the letter.

Attila announced that he considered Honoria's letter and ring a *proposal* of marriage. He said he wanted to marry the young princess. As a *dowry*, he demanded half of the Western Roman Empire. Needless to say, Honoria's brother Valentinian III refused this

---

　　阿提拉的侵略从不需要借口。他总是直接开战，夺走他想要的东西。但是这次他找了个借口。西罗马帝国帝王瓦伦提尼安三世的妹妹奥诺丽亚写信给他，信上说她与男仆私通被发现，男仆被处死，自己被软禁起来。她迫切渴望自由，就送封信给阿提拉，恳求他给予帮助。她把戒指装在信封内，以证明那封信是她写的。

　　阿提拉声称他把奥诺丽亚的信和戒指当作是求婚。他说他想娶那位年轻的公主，要求西罗马帝国拿出一半的国土做嫁妆。毫无疑问，奥诺丽亚的哥哥瓦伦提尼安三世拒绝了这个无理的要求。阿提拉接着就宣称，他将用武力夺走那些应该属于他的东西。

---

romance　*n.*　风流韵事　　　　　　execute　*v.*　将……处死
proposal　*n.*　求婚　　　　　　　　dowry　*n.*　嫁妆；陪嫁

demand. Attila then declared that he would take what was rightfully his by force.

Attila really didn't care about Honoria. It was the Roman lands and riches he wanted. He was determined to get them. He *assembled* an army of about 100,000 men, including both Huns and Germanic allies. In early 451, Attila and his army crossed the Rhine River into Gaul—modern-day France. For several months, the attackers sacked and burned every city they conquered. They killed men, women, and children without mercy. They took people's riches and all their food. Attila believed that nothing could stop him. He was about to get a big surprise.

The Last of the Romans

The Roman Empire was *fortunate* that it still had one great

阿提拉根本不在乎奥诺丽亚，他想要的是罗马的国土和财富，并发誓要将其据为己有。他集结了一支约10万人的军队，其中包括匈奴人和日耳曼盟军。451年年初，阿提拉和他的军队渡过莱茵河，进入高卢——今天的法国。几个月以来，他们所到之处，烧杀抢掠，无恶不作。他们残忍地杀戮，男女老少无一幸免，此外还抢走人们的财物和所有的食物。阿提拉相信什么都阻止不了他，但他却要大吃一惊了。

最后的罗马人

幸运的是罗马帝国还有一位伟大的将军，叫弗拉维斯·埃提乌斯，在

---

assemble *v.* （使）集合；聚集　　　　fortunate *adj.* 侥幸的；幸运的

general. His name was Flavius Aetius, and he served in the court of Valentinian III. He is usually just called Aetius. As the Western Empire *crumbled*, Aetius did all he could to hold the empire together. For his efforts, he has been remembered as "the Last of the Romans".

With the advance of Attila through Gaul, Aetius was facing the greatest test of his life. He scrambled to raise an army. Arguing that Attila was the enemy of *humanity*, Aetius convinced some of the Germanic tribes living in Gaul to join forces with him. These new allies included a large force of Visigoths under the command of their king, Theodoric. Aetius's army was now about as large as Attila's. In the late spring of 451, the Roman general led his forces to fight Attila and the Huns.

瓦伦提尼安三世的皇室供职。通常人们就直接叫他埃提乌斯。当西罗马帝国瓦解时，埃提乌斯竭尽全力护住帝国。他的努力使他作为"最后的罗马人"流芳百世。

阿提拉取道高卢继续进发，而埃提乌斯正面临着他人生中最重大的挑战。他好不容易才凑集了一支军队。他说服一些定居在高卢的日耳曼部落与他联手，理由就是阿提拉毫无人性。这些新的盟友包括在国王狄奥多里克指挥下的一支西哥特人的大部队。现在两军人数旗鼓相当。451年春末，埃提乌斯将军带领着他的军队同阿提拉的匈奴军队展开了激战。

---

crumble *v.* 瓦解   humanity *n.* 人性；人道

Thinking

Critically Aetius needed a larger army to fight the Huns so he convinced men from Gaul to join the Roman army. Which is more important when fighting an enemy?

Number of men or *talent*?

The Battle of Chalons

Aetius and his army *caught up with* Attila in late June outside the city of Orleans, in modern-day France. The Hun army had been conducting a siege of the city. Seeing the approaching Roman forces, Attila retreated toward an open plain near the town of Chalons-sur-Marne. There, the two huge armies met in one of the greatest battles in history.

想一想

埃提乌斯需要一支更庞大的军队来对抗匈奴人，因此他说服来自高卢的人加入罗马军队。那么与敌人作战时，哪一个更为重要呢？

是人数，还是人才？

沙隆之战

六月末，埃提乌斯的军队在奥尔良城（位于今天法国境内）外追上了阿提拉。匈奴人一直在围攻这座城市。看到罗马军队逐渐逼近，阿提拉撤退到靠近沙隆的一片开阔的平原上。两支大军在此交战，此战被视为历史上最重大的战争之一。

---

talent *n.* 天资；才能；人才   catch up with 追上；赶上

The Battle of Chalons began in the afternoon. After firing arrows at each other, the two sides fought up close with swords, spears, and axes. By evening, when the fighting stopped, tens of thousands of men from both sides lay dead on the field. Among them was Theodoric. But there was no question about who had won. Aetius's army had defeated Attila.

The Visigoth king Theodoric was *slain* in battle with Attila and the Huns, but Aetius and the Roman and Visigoth armies went on to beat the Huns.

The next day, Aetius allowed Attila to retreat with the remainder of his army. The Roman general was criticized for this. But Aetius probably made a *wise* decision. His *strategy* was to keep the Germanic forces as allies of Rome. The best way to do this was if

---

沙隆之战在午后开始。双方先是互射火箭，然后开始用剑、长矛和斧头近距离作战。到傍晚战斗结束时，已是横尸遍野，狄奥多里克阵亡。但是此战结果显而易见，埃提乌斯的军队打败了阿提拉。

西哥特国国王狄奥多里克在和阿提拉及匈奴人的战斗中阵亡，但是埃提乌斯和罗马军队还有西哥特军队继续同匈奴人作战。

第二天，埃提乌斯允许阿提拉带着残余部队撤退，他也因此受到了指责。但是埃提乌斯可能做了一个很明智的决定。他的战略目标是维持日耳曼军队与罗马的盟友关系，最好的办法就是让哥特人和罗马人将匈奴人视

---

slay v. 杀死
strategy n. 策略；战略；行动计划

wise adj. （人）充满智慧的；英明的

the Goths and the Romans had the Huns as a common enemy.

Attila's army *withdrew* from Gaul, moving back across the Rhine River to settlement. The Western Roman Empire was safe for the time being. But Attila still had plenty of men, and he hadn't given up on conquering the Western Empire. The Romans hadn't seen the last of Attila and the Huns.

Attila and the Pope

In June of the following year, Attila led his army across the mountains into Italy. He was still pretending that he wanted to marry Honoria.

This time, Aetius was unable to raise an army large enough to fight the Huns. The Germanic people who had helped to save Gaul were less interested in saving Italy. Attila's army *roamed* at will in

---

为共同的敌人。

阿提拉的残部从高卢撤退后，渡过莱茵河安顿下来。西罗马帝国暂时安全了。然而阿提拉仍然拥有大量兵力，并且他也没有放弃征服西罗马帝国。罗马人虽已斩草，却未除根。

阿提拉与教皇

次年六月，阿提拉带领他的军队翻山越岭来到意大利。这次他仍然假装想和奥诺丽亚结婚。

这次，埃提乌斯却无法集结一支足够庞大的军队来对抗匈奴人。帮助解救过高卢的日耳曼民族没有兴趣解救意大利。阿提拉的军队在意大利北

---

withdraw *v.* 撤退

roam *v.* 游荡

northern Italy, *demolishing* villages and killing their inhabitants. The army moved closer and closer toward Rome.

Aetius and Emperor Valentinian decided to try *diplomacy* instead of battle. They asked Pope Leo I, the head of the Catholic Church, for his help. They wanted the pope to meet with Attila and ask him to leave Italy.

Pope Leo met with Attila at the Huns' camp. What the two men said to each other was not recorded. But Attila agreed to stop his attacks.

This victory greatly increased the *prestige* of the pope. However, some historians believe that Attila was in a weaker position than many people realized. They believe his army had not fully recovered

---

部肆无忌惮地毁掉村庄，杀害村民。这支部队正日益向罗马逼近。

埃提乌斯和帝王瓦伦提尼安决定试一试采用外交手段——而非战争——来解决问题。他们向天主教会的领袖——教皇利奥一世求助，希望教皇去会见阿提拉，让他离开意大利。

教皇利奥与阿提拉在匈奴人的营地会见。他们两人的谈话没有被记录下来，但是阿提拉同意了撤军。

这次谈话的结果极大地提高了教皇的声望。然而，有些历史学家们认为，真正的原因是阿提拉没有人们想象的那么强大，他当时是处于弱势地

---

demolish *v.* 摧毁；拆毁
prestige *n.* 声望；威望

diplomacy *n.* 外交；外交手腕

from the Battle of Chalons, and many of his men were dying of a plague. In addition, he was running short of food and other supplies. Whatever Attila's reasons were, he left Italy, never to return.

Divided They Fall

Attila stopped pretending to need Honoria as *bride*. In fact, he already had a number of wives. In AD 453 he took a new bride, a beautiful young woman named Ildico. After a day of feasting, Attila and Ildico went to bed.

The next morning, Attila failed to *emerge* from his bedroom. Worried servants entered his room and found Ildico *trembling* with fear. On the bed lay Attila. He was dead. During the night, the king

---

位。他们认为阿提拉的军队还没有完全从沙隆之战中恢复过来，还有许多士兵死于瘟疫。此外，他正面临着食物短缺和其他供应品匮乏。不管出于什么原因，阿提拉离开了意大利，再也没有回来。

分裂则衰

阿提拉不再假装要娶奥诺丽亚了。事实上，他已经有了一大群妻子。公元453年，他娶了一位新娘，一个名叫伊笛可的年轻貌美的女人。阿提拉和伊笛可结束了一天的盛宴后，上床休息。

第二天早上，阿提拉却没能从床上起来。仆人担心地走进卧室，看到伊笛可惊恐地颤抖着。阿提拉躺在床上，已经死了。前夜，阿提拉的鼻子

---

bride *n.* 新娘
tremble *v.* 发抖；战栗

emerge *v.* 出现

THE UNFORGETTABLE JOURNEY

had suffered a burst blood vessel in his nose or throat. He drowned to death on his own blood.

After the death of Attila, the Huns' empire did not last. His numerous sons split the empire among themselves. Under Attila, the Huns had been united, but now they became divided. Their lack of unity caused them to grow weak.

Germanic tribes that had been ruled by Attila saw that the Huns were weakening. In 454, they *revolted*. Within a few years, they had overthrown the Huns. With their empire shattered, the Huns fled. In the words of one historian, they were "scattered to the winds." Once the terror of humanity, the Huns made no more lasting marks on history.

More than 1,500 years after Attila's reign, people in Hungary asked the government there to officially recognize their *ethnicity* as Hun.

或喉管的某个血管破裂，他溺死在自己的鲜血之中。

阿提拉死后，匈奴帝国名存实亡。他的儿子们分割了这个庞大的帝国。在阿提拉的统治下，匈奴人团结一致；但现在他们四分五裂，逐渐走向了衰落。

曾经处在阿提拉统治下的日耳曼部落眼见匈奴人日渐衰落，454年，他们奋起反抗，短短几年就推翻了匈奴人的统治。帝国灭亡，匈奴人落荒而逃。用一位历史学家的话来说，他们"随风而散"了。除了灭绝人性的残暴，匈奴人没有在历史上留下什么更持久的印记了。

在阿提拉统治的1 500年后，匈牙利人民要求当地政府正式认可他们为"匈奴民族"。

---

revolt *v.* 反叛；造反

ethnicity *n.* 种族地位